About the Author

EUGENE EHRLICH, formerly a member of the department of English and Comparative Literature at Columbia University, is the author of numerous reference books on language, including *Amo, Amas, Amat and More* and *The Highly Selective Thesaurus for the Extraordinarily Literate*. He is also the coeditor of *The New Oxford American Dictionary*.

About the Editor

MARGARET A. BRUCIA earned her Ph.D. in Classics from Fordham University and is a Fellow of the American Academy in Rome. After teaching high-school Latin for many years on Long Island, she now teaches in the Classics Department at Temple University's Rome campus during the spring semester.

VENI, VIDI, VICI

VENI, VIDI, VICI

Second Edition

*Conquer Your Enemies and
Impress Your Friends with
Everyday Latin*

EUGENE EHRLICH

Revised and Updated by Margaret A. Brucia

HARPER

NEW YORK • LONDON • TORONTO • SYDNEY

HARPER

VENI, VIDI, VICI. Copyright © 1995, 2010 by the Estate of Eugene Ehrlich.
All rights reserved. Printed in the United States of America. No part of
this book may be used or reproduced in any manner whatsoever without
written permission except in the case of brief quotations embodied in critical articles and reviews. For information address HarperCollins Publishers,
10 East 53rd Street, New York, NY 10022.

HarperCollins books may be purchased for educational, business, or sales
promotional use. For information please write: Special Markets Department, HarperCollins Publishers, 10 East 53rd Street, New York, NY 10022.

First Quill/HarperResource edition published 2001.
First Harper paperback published 2010.

Designed by Alma Orenstein

The Library of Congress has catalogued the first edition as follows:

Ehrlich, Eugene H.
    Veni vidi vici : / conquer your enemies, impress your friends with
everyday Latin / Eugene Ehrlich.
        p.   cm.
    "A Hudson Group book."
    Includes index.
    ISBN 0-06-273365-6
    1. English language—Foreign words and phrases—Latin—
Dictionaries.   2. Proverbs, Latin—Translations into English.
3. Maxims, Latin—Translations into English.   4. Latin language—
Terms and phrases.   I. Title.
PE1582.L3E38   1995
422'.471—dc20   94-42354

ISBN 978-0-06-176803-3 (second edition)

---

10   11   12   13   14   /RRD   10   9   8   7   6   5   4   3   2   1

To Sam, Mickey, Hazel, Rebecca, Margie,
Alice, Harry, and Ruth

veni I came
vidi I saw
vici I conquered

. . .

—the best-known Latin sentence of
them all, freely rendered as "a piece of
cake," reported by Plutarch to have
been uttered by Julius Caesar when
announcing his victory in 47 B.C. over
Pharnaces, king of Pontus.

Contents

Foreword

I have revered Eugene Ehrlich's learned and entertaining compendia of Latin expressions since they were first published. When I taught high-school Latin, I kept copies of *Amo, Amas, Amat* and *Veni, Vidi, Vici* in my classroom. Eugene's volumes were the ideal source for the right Latin expression to suit any situation or occasion. Even though I never met Eugene Ehrlich, I knew that he was a *rara avis* (RAAH-rah AH-wihs) whose scholarly acumen rivaled his sage and sometimes trenchant humor.

Shortly before Eugene's death in the spring of 2008, his son Henry asked for my thoughts about revising *Veni, Vidi, Vici* for republication and put me in touch with Stephanie Meyers at HarperCollins. I suggested a revision of the pronunciation guide. Some entries, it seemed to me, would benefit from a bit of gentle tweaking to broaden the scope of the audience: Eugene had a penchant for addressing like-minded coevals. Updating several of the references to the modern world also seemed necessary because *Veni, Vidi, Vici* was first published in 1995.

With the support and encouragement of Henry Ehrlich and Stephanie Meyers, the task of revising *Veni, Vidi, Vici* has become a labor of love. It has allowed me to wrestle with some knotty problems of pronunciation and to savor again, and at a slower pace, some of the pithiest and most perceptive Latin gems. But perhaps the most challenging aspect of this project has been to follow my own mandate: to keep all the entries true to the inimitable flavor of Eugene's originals, both in style and content. In that, above all, I hope I have succeeded.

I will consider my labor fruitful if, as a result, the wisdom of Eugene and his cohort of Latin authors reaches a wide circle of new admirers. This book is intended not only for students and teachers of Latin and classical antiquity, toast makers and speech writers, linguists and word enthusiasts, but for everyone, old and young, who takes delight in being reminded that *nihil sub sole novi* (NIH-hihl suub SOH-leh NAW-wee): there's nothing new under the sun. My fondest hope is that *Veni, Vidi, Vici* may even inspire some of its readers to pursue the study of Latin.

MARGARET A. BRUCIA

Preface to the First Edition

Amo, Amas, Amat and More, the predecessor of *Veni, Vidi, Vici*, has remained in print both at home and abroad since it was first published by HarperCollins in 1985. Since that time, my interest in collecting interesting and useful Latin expressions has not flagged. Some of the words and phrases I've collected were provided by readers of *Amo, Amas, Amat and More*, others by my continuing reading of authors who write in English but express themselves in Latin from time to time. My files of Latin expressions finally reached a critical mass over a year ago, and the present volume began to take form. It is my hope that *Veni, Vidi, Vici* will prove at least as entertaining and instructive for readers—judging by letters I have received—as *Amo, Amas, Amat and More*.

In the present volume the reader will find only a few of the entries that appeared in *Amo, Amas, Amat and More* but in every case such phrases are subsumed under new entries to which they are related in meaning. Thus, whenever a reader wonders why I have not included phrases known to that reader, one explanation is that I did not want to repeat wholesale the entry list of *Amo, Amas, Amat and More*. Of course, another explanation is that I have been remiss in *Veni, Vidi, Vici*.

As in the previous volume, the attempt is made in many entries of this book to supply enlightening free translations as well as literal explanations. Again as in the previous volume, most of the entries in this book date back to classical times, but there is some treatments of phrases that came into use long after the decline of the Roman Empire. It will be seen that this book presents a greater proportion of maxims and proverbs than are found in its predecessor, but the criteria for inclusion remain the same—the inherent wisdom reflected in the thought presented and the insight the entries provide into a civilization that still captures modern imagination.

Now to repeat a few words from *Amo, Amas, Amat and More* about the pronunciations supplied in this book. No one knows just how Latin was pronounced by the Romans. I was taught by my instructors at Townsend Harris High School and the City College of New York to pronounce the name *Caesar* as though the first letter were a *k*. Others may pronounce that first letter as though it were *ch*, as in *chew*. This difference, along with several other questions of pronunciation, is moot. Let me assure the reader, however, that using the pronunciations offered in this book will make it possible to pronounce Latin without incurring the scorn of most people who have studied the language in American public schools.

Eugene Ehrlich

Pronunciation Notes

This volume uses a respelling scheme to represent the sounds of Latin. Stresses are indicated by typographic means.

Stress. Stressed syllables are shown in capital letters, and unstressed syllables, as well as words of a single syllable, are shown in lower case. Thus *ego* (I) is pronounced EH-gaw, *virtūs* (virtue) is pronounced WIHR-toos, and *ars* (art) is pronounced ahrs.

Syllabification. The rules of Latin syllabification are complex and inconsistent. Evidence from Latin poetry and from inscriptions informs us that syllables usually begin with a consonant or a combination of pronounceable consonants. Prefixes, however, remain intact and form separate syllables. An *x* is placed in the same syllable as the preceding vowel.

Macrons. A macron is a mark (–), sometimes called a long mark, placed above a Latin vowel to distinguish long from short vowels. A long vowel takes twice as much time to say as a short vowel. In the cases of *e, i, o,* and *u,* both the sound of the vowel and the length of time required to pronounce it depend on whether the vowel is long or short. In the case of *a,* however, only the length of the vowel is affected; the sound remains the same whether the *a* is long or short. Macrons are helpful for correct pronunciation but are not generally used in written Latin.

Vowels. Like English vowels, certain Latin vowels have various qualities (sound) and quantities (length). The samples given in the chart below help in sounding out the Latin words on the pages that follow.

Vowel	Pronunciation		English Word	Latin Word	Latin Pronunciation
short *a*	AH *or* ah	*as in*	far	*parō*	PAH-roh
long *a*	AAH or aah	*as in*	father	*cārus*	KAAH-ruus
short *e*	EH *or* eh	*as in*	set	*petere*	PEH-teh-reh
long *e*	AY *or* ay	*as in*	gray	*fēcit*	FAY-kiht
short *i*	IH *or* ih	*as in*	dip	*id*	ihd
long *i*	EE *or* ee	*as in*	sweet	*vīta*	WEE-tah
short *o*	AW *or* aw	*as in*	often	*hominem*	HAW-mih-nehm
long *o*	OH *or* oh	*as in*	both	*dōnō*	DOH-noh
short *u*	UU *or* uu	*as in*	put	*nunc*	nuunk
long *u*	OO or oo	*as in*	rude	*ūna*	OO-nah

Additional information about vowels. When two discrete vowels (or a vowel and a diphthong) are juxtaposed in Latin, a transitional sound is added for ease of pronunciation. For example, the sound of the English *y* acts as a transition between short *e* and short *u,* as in *meus* (my), pronounced MEH-yuus, or between short *i* and short *u,* as in *gladius* (sword), pronounced GLAH-dih-yuus. Similarly, the sound of the English *w* acts as a transition between two short *u*'s, as in *tuus* (your), pronounced TUU-wuus, or between short *u* and long *i,* as in *fuī* (I have been), pronounced FUU-wee.

After the letter *q,* and sometimes after *g* and *s,* the Latin *u* has the sound of the English *w.* This is no surprise for speakers of English. Consider the words *quick, guava,* and *suave.* Thus, *quandōque* (whenever) is pronounced kwahn-DOH-kweh, and *suāve* (pleasant) is pronounced SWAAH-weh.

The letter *y* is not found in the Latin alphabet but does appear in a few Latin words borrowed from Greek. In all occurrences in this book, *y*'s serve as short vowels. Although there is no sound in English that accurately represents the sound of *y* in Greek or Latin, we can approximate the sound of short *y* by pronouncing the *y* as *ü* in the German word *über.*

Diphthongs. Like English, in which, for example, the diphthong *oi* is given a single sound (as in *point)* and *ou* is given a single sound (as in *loud),* Latin has its share of diphthongs.

When the second vowel in the combinations *eī, oē,* and *uī* is long, these vowels are not pronounced as diphthongs and each

Diphthong	Pronunciation		English Word	Latin Word	Latin Pronunciation
ae	Ī or ī	*as in*	my	*Caesar*	KĪ-sahr
au	OW *or* ow	*as in*	now	*Augustus*	ow-GUUS-tuus
ei	EY *or* ey	*as in*	grey	*deinde*	DEYN-deh
eu	EHYOO *or* ehyoo*	*as in*	feud	*ēheu*	AY-hehyoo
oe	OY *or* oy	*as in*	boy	*proelium*	PROY-lih-yuum
ui	OOWEE *or* oowee*	*as in*	phooey	*cui*	koowee

*Pronounce quickly as a single sound.

vowel has a separate sound, as in the Latin words *deī* (DEH-yee), *poēta* (paw-WAY-tah), and *suī* (SUU-wee).

Consonants. Latin consonants are generally pronounced in the same way as their English equivalents, with the following more notable exceptions:

- The Latin *c* is pronounced as though it were a *k*. Thus *Cicero* is pronounced KIH-keh-roh.
- The Latin *g* is pronounced like the *g* in the English word *give*. Thus, *gemma* (gem) is pronounced GEHM-mah.
- A *j* is often seen before a vowel in some Latin texts where one would expect to see an *i*. Whichever letter is used, the sound is taken as an initial *y*, as in the English word *young*. This means that the *i* (as well as the *j*) functions as a consonant. Thus, the Latin word for *justice,* whether spelled *iūs* or *jūs,* is pronounced yoos, but when *i* appears before a consonant, it is pronounced as a vowel. As speakers of modern languages, we are not dismayed by such apparent anomalies. Consider the pronunciation of the English word *union* (initial syllable pronounced YOON) and that of the English word *unable* (initial syllable pronounced uun).
- The Latin *r* is trilled.
- The Latin *s* is always pronounced like the *s* in the English word *set* or *pets*. Thus *semper parātus* (always ready) is pronounced SEHM-pehr pah-RAAH-tuus.
- The Latin *v* is always pronounced as though it were a *w*. Thus, *avē atque valē* is pronounced AH-way AHT-kweh WAH-lay.
- The Latin consonant *x* is considered a double consonant

and has the sound of *ks,* as it does in English. Thus the Latin word *ex* (out of) is pronounced *ehks.*

- The combinations of the letters *ch, ph,* and *th* reflect a Greek origin and are not pronounced as they are normally pronounced in English. The initial consonant is aspirated, as in the English words *chaos, uphill,* and *Thailand.* Thus, the Latin word *chorda* (chord) is pronounced KHAWR-dah. Similarly, the Latin words *philosophus* (philosopher) and *thēsaurus* (treasure) are pronounced phih-LAW-saw-phuus and thay-SOW-ruus, with aspirated *p*'s and *t.*

A final note on pronunciation. The difficulty of reconstructing the correct pronunciation of a language that is no longer spoken cannot be overestimated. Ascertaining the quantities of particular vowels (in other words, whether they are "long" or "short") is often a vexing issue that has brought many linguistic scholars to the point of verbal fisticuffs. Dictionaries are not always helpful (as the quantities of vowels are not always indicated) and, indeed, are often contradictory. This pronunciation guide may not satisfy the demanding requirements of serious scholars and linguists, but it will more than suffice for those enthusiasts and students who strive to pronounce Classical Latin both intelligibly and intelligently.

Dramatis Personae
(DRAAH-mah-tihs pehr-SOH-nī)
List of Characters

Apuleius. *Lucius Apuleius.* Flourished around A.D. 155. Born and lived most of his life in northern Africa. Best remembered for his work entitled *Metamorphoses*, also known as *The Golden Ass*, a Latin novel in eleven books, the most famous episode of which is the story of Cupid and Psyche.

Caesar. *Gaius Iulius Caesar.* 100–44 B.C. Born at Rome. Soldier, statesman. *Bellum Gallicum* (*The Gallic War*), *Bellum civile* (*The Civil War*).

Cardinal Newman. *Venerable John Henry (Cardinal) Newman.* 1801–1890. Born in London, England. A prolific and influential Roman Catholic priest and cardinal who converted to Catholicism from Anglicanism in 1845. He was declared "Venerable" by the Catholic Church in 1991, a step toward attaining canonization as a saint.

Catullus. *Gaius Valerius Catullus.* 84?–54? B.C. Born at Verona, in Cisalpine Gaul. Best known for his tempestuous love affair with a Roman gentlewoman (probably the notorious Clodia), whom he immortalized in his poems under the pseudonym Lesbia. *Carmina* (*Poems*).

Cicero. *Marcus Tullius Cicero.* 106–43 B.C. Born at Arpinum in central Italy. Jurist, statesman, writer, philosopher. *Orationes* (*Orations*), *Rhetorica* (*Writings on Rhetoric*), *Philosophica* (*Political and Philosophical Writings*), *Epistulae* (*Letters*).

Claudian. *Claudius Claudianus.* A.D. 4th cent.–c. 404. From Alexandria. A speaker of Greek. Came to Italy and mastered Latin, which was the language of his writings. Court poet under the emperor Honorius; his poetry eulogized his patrons. *De consulatu Honorii* (*On the Consulship of Honorius*), *De consolatu Stilichonis* (*On the Consulship of Stilicho*).

Descartes. *René Descartes* (also known as *Renatus Cartesius*). 1596–1650. Born in France, died in Sweden, and buried in Paris. Philosopher, mathematician, scientist, and writer who spent most of his adult life in the Dutch Republic. Hailed today as the father of both modern philosophy and analytic geometry, in 1663 the Pope placed his works on the Index of Prohibited Books.

Ennius. *Quintus Ennius.* 239–169 B.C. Born in Calabria, Italy. Served in the Roman army and was awarded Roman citizenship. A prolific writer, whose work survives only in fragmentary form. His principal works were tragedies and the *Annales,* a sweeping history of Rome, written in dactylic hexameter, from its origins to his own day. Ennius was regarded as the father of Latin literature.

Gregory the Great. c. A.D. 540–604. Born in Rome. Pope from A.D. 590 until his death, Gregory was one of the six Latin Fathers of the Church and the first pope to come from a monastic background. He was canonized a saint by the Catholic Church and was admired by John Calvin. He wrote the *Dialogues,* an account of the life of his master, St. Benedict, and other saints of the period.

Horace. *Quintus Horatius Flaccus.* 65–8 B.C. Born at Venusia, in southern Italy. Member of the literary circle brought together by Maecenas under the patronage of the emperor Augustus. *Carmina* (*Odes*), *Epodi* (*Epodes*), *Satirae* (*Satires*), *Epistulae* (*Verse Letters*), *Ars Poetica* (*The Poetic Art*).

Juvenal. *Decimus Iunius Iuvenalis.* A.D. 1st–2nd cent. Born at Aquinum, Italy. Author of verse satires attacking the corruption of Roman society. *Satirae* (*Satires*).

Livy. *Titus Livius.* 59 B.C.–A.D. 17 or 64 B.C.–A.D. 12. Born at Patavium, now Padua, in northeastern Italy. Historian. *Ab urbe condita* ([History of Rome] *from the Founding of the City*).

Lucan. *Marcus Annaeus Lucanus.* A.D. 39–65. Born at Cordoba, in Spain. Courtier in the reign of Nero. Fell from grace and eventually was forced to commit suicide after becoming implicated in the Pisonian conspiracy. *Pharsalia* (a poetic account of Rome's civil war).

Lucretius. *Titus Lucretius Carus.* Prob. 94–55 B.C. Probably member of an aristocratic family, the Lucretii. Poet and philosopher. *De rerum natura* (*On the Nature of the Universe*).

Manilius. *Marcus Manilius.* 1st cent B.C.–A.D. 1st cent. Facts of his life are unknown. *Astronomica* (a didactic poem on astrology).

Marcus Aurelius. *Marcus Aurelius Antoninus.* A.D. 121–180. Roman emperor. *Meditationes* (*Meditations*).

Martial. *Marcus Valerius Martialis.* C. A.D. 40–C. 104. Born at Bilbilis, in Spain. Depicted Roman society in epigrammatic verse. *Epigrammata* (*Epigrams*).

Ovid. *Publius Ovidius Naso.* 43 B.C.–A.D. 17. Born at Sulmo, in central Italy. Intended by his father for a legal career, but gave it up to devote himself to poetry. Member of the literary circle of Messalla. Exiled to the Black Sea by Augustus, who was offended by Ovid's poetry, though there may have been other offenses as well. *Amores* (*Love Poems*), *Ars Amatoria* (*The Amatory Art*), *Metamorphoses* (*Changes*).

Persius. *Aulus Persius Flaccus.* A.D. 34–62. Born at Volaterrae, in northern Italy. Stoic satirist. *Satirae* (*Satires*).

Phaedrus. C. 15 B.C.–C. A.D. 50. A Thracian, born a slave. Eventually became a freedman in the household of the emperor Augustus. *Fabulae* (*Fables*).

Plautus. *Titus Maccius Plautus.* 3rd–2nd cent. B.C. Born at Sarsina, in central Italy. Author of comic dramas based on Greek originals.

Pliny the Elder. *Gaius Plinius.* A.D. 23/4–79. Born at Comum, now Como, in north-central Italy. Military commander in Germany, provincial administrator, counselor to emperors Vespasian and Titus. *Naturalis historia* (*Natural History*).

Publilius Syrus. 1st cent. B.C. Came to Rome as a slave, perhaps from Antioch. Author of mimes. *Sententiae* (*Maxims*).

Quintilian. *Marcus Fabius Quintilianus.* C. A.D. 30–before 100. Born at Calagurris, in Spain. Teacher of rhetoric; among his pupils was Pliny the Younger. *Institutio oratoria* (*The Teaching of Oratory*).

Sallust. *Gaius Sallustius Crispus.* 86–35 B.C. A Roman politician turned historian after he was expelled from the senate, probably on trumped-up charges against his character. He wrote three historical monographs, two of which, *Bellum*

Catilinae and *Bellum Jugurthinum*, survive. A third, *Historiae*, exists in fragmentary form.

Seneca the Younger. *Lucius Annaeus Seneca*. Between 4 and 1 B.C.–A.D. 65. Born at Cordoba, in Spain. Counselor to Nero, philosopher, poet. *Dialogi* (*Dialogues*), *Naturales quaestiones* (*Natural Questions*, inquiries in physical science), *Apocolocyntosis* (*The Pumpkinification* [of the emperor Claudius]), tragedies, epigrams.

Suetonius. *Gaius Suetonius Tranquillus*. C. A.D. 69–? Practiced law briefly, held various posts in the imperial service, secretary to the emperor Hadrian. *De vita Caesarum* (*Lives of the Caesars* [from Julius to Domitian]).

Tacitus. *Cornelius Tacitus*. C. 56 A.D.–after 115. Probably from northern Italy or Gaul. Historian, held several official posts. *Annales* (*Annals*), *Historiae* (*Histories*), *Agricola* ([Biography of his father-in-law, Gnaeus Iulius] *Agricola*), *Germania*.

Terence. *Publius Terentius Afer*. C. 190–159 B.C. Born in northern Africa, brought to Rome as a slave. Author of comic dramas adapted from Greek models by Apollodorus of Carystus and Menander. *Andria* (*The Girl from Andros*), *Hecyra* (*The Mother-in-Law*), *Heauton timorumenos* (*The Self-Punisher*), *Eunuchus* (*The Eunuch*), *Phormio*, *Adelphi* (*The Brothers*).

Virgil. *Publius Vergilius Maro*. 70–19 B.C. Born near Mantua, in northeastern Italy. Early in his career deeply influenced by Catullus, member of the literary circle of Asinius Pollio. Later, through Maecenas, came under the patronage of the emperor Augustus. *Aeneid* (an epic poem about the founding of Rome by Aeneas), *Georgics* (a treatise on farming in poetry), *Eclogues* (pastoral poems).

VENI, VIDI, VICI

A

a baculo
aah BAH-kuu-loh
with a big stick

Literally "by means of the rod." The phrase *a baculo* characterizes a threat of force—the big stick—rather than a resort to logic or to sweet talk—the carrot. **Baculum** (BAH-kuu-luum) is a stick or stave, quite useful as a convincer in hand-to-hand encounters, for example, with a night prowler. In international disputes, *baculum* might be a modern fighter-bomber.

ab agendo
ahb ah-GEHN-doh
out of action

For those who prefer more formal language, *ab agendo* can also be translated as "incapacitated." But this phrase can also be taken to mean "retired"—for the extraordinarily literate, "superannuated." A final meaning is "obsolete." Thus, typewriters and typists now may be considered *ab agendo* no matter which translation you use.

ab ante
ahb AHN-teh
in advance

Literally "from before." An apt phrase for those with closed minds: "I didn't have to think. My mind was made up *ab ante*, indeed, even before the debate over where to eat began."

ab antiquo
ahb ahn-TEE-kwoh
from olden times

A phrase, literally "from ancient times," useful for those who are given incurably to looking back to the good old days when . . . "If only life were as uncomplicated today as it was *ab antiquo*!"

abest
AHB-ehst
not present

A term useful in a roll call, literally "he (or she) is absent." A helpful fellow student may employ this effectively when the teacher calls a name and is met with no response. Or the teacher may choose to convert this word to a question by adding the enclitic *-ne*. For example, "**Abestne** (ahb-EHST-neh) Matilda?" ("Is Matilda absent?") To which an overlooked Matilda might respond, "**Adsum**!" (AHD-suum) ("I'm here!")

abeunt studia in mores
AHB-eh-yuunt STOO-dih-yah ihn MOH-rays
you are what you eat

In this maxim from Ovid, literally "pursuits meld into character," we are reminded that our interests, whatever they may be, shape our character. In matters of food consumption, for example, are you more interested in pursuing quality or quantity? Have your dining habits made you a gourmet or a gourmand?

ab hoc et ab hac et ab illa
ahb hohk eht ahb haahk eht ahb IHL-laah
the talk of gossips

This intriguing phrase, literally "from this man, this woman, and that woman," characterizes something heard or said in general gossip, with no indication of its precise source. But the phrase, which can also be translated as "from here, there, and everywhere," may be taken as the equivalent of "indiscriminately" or "confusedly." This is an especially handy phrase for a quick thinker seeking to evade a direct answer to a pesky question posed by an overbearing authority figure or a nosy busybody. "Where did you ever get such an idea?" "*Ab hoc et ab hac et ab illa.*" A perfectly obfuscatory reply!

ab igne ignem
ahb IHG-neh IHG-nehm
as you sow, so shall you reap

Literally "from fire, fire," suggesting that we can expect to get out of something no more and no less than what we put into it. So if we sow dissension, how can we expect to reap anything but further dissension? (See also TIBI SERIS, TIBI METIS and UT SEMENTEM FECERIS, ITA METES.)

abi in pace
AHB-ee ihn PAAH-keh
ciao

Literally "depart in peace," a Latin variant of **vade** (WAAH-deh) **in pace**, "go in peace"—both meaning "good-bye." If more than one person is addressed, the correct phrase is **abite** (ahb-EE-teh) **in pace**.

abiit ad maiores (or majores)
AHB-ih-yiht ahd mah-YOH-rays
he's kicked the bucket

When someone has died, we are accustomed to hearing such euphemisms as "she has passed away" and "he was laid to rest." The Romans did not do much better in *abiit ad maiores*, "he (or she) has gone to the ancestors." And if more than one person has achieved this state, the correct phrase is **abierunt** (ahb-ih-yay-ruunt) **ad maiores**, "they have gone."

abiit, excessit, evasit, erupit
AHB-ih-yiht ehks-KEHS-siht ay-WAAH-siht ay-ROO-piht
he's flown the coop

There's no doubt about what is being said—"he has gone, he has made off, he has escaped, he has broken away." And who is he? Catiline, the profligate Roman noble who conspired in 63 B.C. to overthrow the government of Rome. And who is saying this? Cicero, the Roman statesman and orator, flaunting his eloquence in this sentence of his second oration against Catiline. (For additional information on Catiline's career, see ALIENI APPETENS.)

ab inconvenienti
ahb ihn-kawn-weh-nih-YEHN-tee
from inconvenience

A rhetorical term characterizing an argument—a proof—designed to show that the opposite point of view is untenable because of the inconvenience or hardship it would create. The full phrase designating such a proof is **argumentum** (ahr-goo-MEHN-tuum) **ab inconvenienti**.

ab integro
ahb IHN-teh-groh
anew *or* afresh

This phrase suggests a new beginning, a fresh start. It is appropriate in reference to a change in location, job, relationship, or, for that matter, to any new course of conduct or action. "Let's begin *ab integro* to see whether we can make a better go of it this time."

abnormis sapiens crassaque Minerva
ahb-NOHR-mihs SAH-pih-yayns KRAHS-sah-kweh mih-NEHR-wah
a natural-born philosopher with nothing but horse sense

Horace, in his *Satires,* characterizes someone, literally "an unorthodox sage of rough genius," with valuable insights to offer despite—because of?—a lack of academic training. Horace tells us that this person is uninspired by Minerva, the Roman goddess of wisdom.

absens heres non erit
AHB-sayns HAY-rays nohn EH-riht
absence doesn't make the heart grow fonder

This realistic maxim, "the absent one will not be the heir," cautions against complacency. Anyone who thinks an expected inheritance is in the bag may not pay sufficient attention to a wealthy family member before it is too late to do so. More broadly, it warns the unwary that there's many a slip between cup and lip—a promised political plum may not prove to be a sure thing, and having the inside track for a lucrative contract does not mean one can rest easy until the contract is signed. Intimate knowledge of *absens heres non erit* is what keeps hordes of lobbyists on the job, haunting the halls of Congress especially when an important piece of legislation is being written. Remember that it ain't over till the fat lady sings.

absente reo
ahb-SEHN-teh RAY-yoh
you have to show up

A legal term, "the defendant being absent," suggesting that failure of a defendant to appear in court when summoned can scarcely be considered an indication of innocence.

absolvi meam animam
ahb-SAWL-wee MEH-yahm AH-nih-mahm
there, I got that off my chest

Once you have confessed your peccadillo or even something worse, you may be impelled to say or think *absolvi meam animam,* literally "I have set my mind free." (See also LIBERAVI ANIMAM MEAM.)

absque argento omnia vana
AHBS-kweh ahr-GEHN-toh AWM-nih-yah WAAH-nah
first you must put food on the table

Who will contest this aphorism, literally "without money all efforts are useless"? Not George Bernard Shaw, who went much further: "Lack of money is the root of all evil." And what about Paul, in *Timothy:* "Love of money is the root of all evil"? Could they both have been right?

absque hoc
AHBS-kweh hohk
without this

A legal term used in a formal denial of an allegation. "You have produced no witness to the crime, and *absque hoc* there is no basis for holding my client responsible."

absque ulla conditione
AHBS-kweh OOL-laah kawn-dih-tih-YOH-neh
no ifs, ands, or buts

Literally "without any condition." When one surrenders *absque ulla conditione*—whether to a superior military force or to the strength of authority or to moral suasion—nothing is to be held back. "You will have that report on my desk at close of business today *absque ulla conditione.*" No excuses will be tolerated, no conditions, no reservations. And that's the way the real world works.

abundans cautela non nocet
ah-BUUN-daahns kow-TAY-lah nohn NAW-keht
you can't be too careful

Literally "abundant caution does no harm." In general, being told to look before you leap is good advice, but if we look too many times before we leap, we may find that a golden opportunity has passed us by.

abundant dulcibus vitiis
ah-BUUN-dahnt DUUL-kih-buus WIH-tih-yees
nobody's perfect

An indulgent characterization, literally "they abound with lovely faults," from Quintilian, who knew and enjoyed an engaging foible when he encountered one. (See also VITIIS NEMO SINE NASCITUR.)

ab universali ad particulare valet, a particulari ad universale non valet consequentia
ahb oo-nih-wehr-SAAH-lee ahd pahr-tih-kuu-LAAH-reh WAH-leht aah pahr-tih-kuu-LAAH-ree ahd oo-nih-wehr-SAAH-leh nohn WAH-leht kohn-seh-KWEHN-tih-yah
let's get our logic straight

We reason logically when we apply a general truth—but let's be sure the general truth is universally correct—about a group to individual members of that group: *ab universali ad particulare valet*, "inference from the universal to the particular is valid." Thus, it is a valid syllogism to state, "All A is C, all B is A, therefore all B is C." But dangerous stereotyping can result from the logical error of reasoning from the particular to the general: *a particulari ad universale non valet consequentia*, "inference from the particular to the universal is not valid." Many faulty attitudes are the result of backwards or syllogistically faulty reasoning: "He's a member of X group, he is a terrible person, therefore all members of X group are terrible persons." Watch out.

a caelo usque ad centrum
aah KĪ-loh UUS-kweh ahd KEHN-truum
property rights

A phrase in real estate deeds defining the extent of a landowner's holdings, literally "from heaven to the center." That is, while a deed will surely spell out the length and breadth of the property, what about the space above it and the land beneath it? What part of these does the landowner own? The answer is quite clear, *a caelo usque ad centrum,* everything above the land and everything below it—all the way to the center of the earth. Today we may speak of "air rights" and "mineral rights." A pale imitation of "from heaven to the center of the earth."

acceptissima semper munera sunt auctor quae pretiosa facit

ahk-kayp-TIHS-sih-mah SEHM-pehr MOO-neh-rah suunt OWK-tawr kwī preh-tih-YOH-sah FAH-kiht

it's the thought behind a gift that counts

An aphorism from Ovid, more literally "most acceptable always are the gifts that the giver makes precious." In this age of online gift registries, the donor often does little more than determine the appropriate amount to spend on the donee. A quick click reasonably ensures that a suitable gift will be speedily sent on its way. No muss, no fuss. What would Ovid have to say about this?

accusare nemo se debet, nisi coram deo

ahk-koo-SAAH-reh NAY-moh say DAY-beht NIH-sih KOH-rahm DEH-yoh

taking the Fifth

A phrase in law, "no one is bound to accuse himself (or herself) unless before God." This is one of the human rights spelled out in the U.S. Bill of Rights, Article V of which includes the words "nor shall be compelled in any criminal case to be a witness against himself." Article V is generally known as the Fifth Amendment, and the process of invoking the Fifth Amendment to refuse to answer possibly self-incriminating questions before a grand jury, in court testimony, or in other sworn official interrogations is known informally as "taking the Fifth." In the phrase *nisi coram deo,* "unless before God," the full Latin formulation does not rule out the possibility of answering fully to a higher authority.

ac etiam
ahk EH-tih-yahm
and also *or* and even

acti labores iucundi (or jucundi)
AAHK-tee lah-BOH-rays yoo-KUUN-dee
satisfaction in a job well done

The phrase *acti labores iucundi,* "completed chores are pleasant," was a common maxim even in Cicero's day. If long-distance runners dwelled on the pain of performance more than they basked in the glory of accomplishment, would there be a Boston marathon?

actio personalis moritur cum persona
AAHK-tih-yoh pehr-soh-NAAH-lihs MAW-rih-tuur kuum pehr-SOH-naah
dead men don't sue

A legal principle, "a personal action dies with the person," stemming from common law, the unwritten law based on custom or earlier court decisions. Thus—in certain courts, at least—a personal suit undertaken against another is voided when the plaintiff dies.

actum agere
AAHK-tuum AH-geh-reh
to beat a dead horse

Literally, "to do what has already been done." A useful phrase in any number of situations involving the uselessness and futility of repetition. It is *actum agere* to continue to force your point of view on people who will never see it your way; it is *actum agere* to revise your work to excess; it is *actum agere* to plagiarize; it is even *actum agere* to serve reheated leftovers for dinner.

actum est de republica
AAHK-tuum ehst day ray-POO-blih-kaah
it's all over for us

Many among us, alarmists by nature, are quick to give up on government and society when things appear to be going badly. Of course, Chicken Littles sometimes prove correct—the sky is indeed falling. Such was the case with the once-powerful Roman empire, when the statement *actum est de republica*, literally "it's all over with the commonwealth," proved to be true. When we contemplate making alarming pronouncements, it behooves us nevertheless to think twice before unduly alarming the unwary. Maybe, after all, the sky is not really falling. (But maybe it is.)

actus dei nemini facit iniuriam (or injuriam)
AAHK-tuus DEH-yee NAY-mih-nee FAH-kiht ihn-YOO-rih-yahm

sorry, we have to reject your claim

This is the "act of God" principle, literally "an act of God injures nobody," which gets insurance companies off the hook when property or lives are damaged, for example, by abnormal tides, earthquakes, lightning, or storms. The idea is that such natural phenomena are beyond the control of ordinary mortals and so are not covered by insurance. Please look carefully at the fine print the next time you consider taking out a policy.

actus me invito factus non est meus actus
AAHK-tuus may ihn-WEE-toh FAHK-tuus nohn ehst MEH-yuus AAHK-tuus
I was only following orders

A legal phrase, literally "an act done against my will is not my act," that makes life difficult for police officers and prosecuting attorneys. In conformity with this principle, if a person is coerced into signing an agreement, committing a crime, or confessing guilt, the law does not hold the person responsible.

a cuspide corona
aah KUUS-pih-deh kaw-ROH-nah
the way to get ahead

Conventional wisdom has it that every young man or woman enrolling at West Point dreams of one day becoming President of the United States. Thus, we are not surprised to see in *a cuspide corona*, literally "from the spear a crown," that in Rome successful military service surely helped in reaching the top of the republic.

ad bivium
ahd BIH-wih-yuum
at the crossroads

More literally and charmingly "at a place where two ways meet." To paraphrase Yogi Berra, "If you find yourself *ad bivium*, take it." In antiquity a **trivium** (TRIH-wih-yuum), or an intersection of three roads, was a natural meeting spot and, as such, was commonly equipped with benches for travelers. As people waited for their friends or simply rested, they passed the time by engaging in small talk or conversations on *trivial* subjects.

ad crumenam
ahd kruu-MAY-nahm
the promise of a payday for someone

A phrase, literally "to the purse," used in **argumentum** (ahr-goo-MEHN-tuum) **ad crumenam**, "an appeal based on the possibility of profit." This is an almost surefire way to convince someone to go along with you in what you propose—there's profit in it for both of us. *Argumentum ad crumenam* makes for success in negotiation.

ad extremum
ahd ehks-TRAY-muum
at last

The noun *extremum* may also be translated as "the extreme," and in the phrase **ad extremum virium** (WEE-rih-yuum), "of powers," gives us "to the utmost of one's powers." Thus, if we wish to encourage someone to go all out in pursuing a goal, we can say, "Never give up. Work *ad extremum virium.*"

ad fidelis
ahd fih-DAY-lees
to the faithful

When we preach to the choir or address an audience of those who need no converting to our cause, we are speaking *ad fidelis.* Fund-raisers for a particular political party or organization, for example, would probably save postage by targeting their appeal *ad fidelis.*

ad finem
ahd FEE-nehm
to the end

This phrase can also be translated as "at the end" and "finally," as in "I wish *ad finem* to thank you for listening so politely to my interminable commencement address." In the phrase **ad finem fidelis** (fih-DAY-lees), we have "faithful to the end," a perfect epitaph for a beloved pet.

adhibenda est in iocando (or jocando) moderatio
ahd-hih-BEHN-dah ehst ihn yaw-KAHN-doh maw-deh-RAAH-tih-yoh
try not to offend people with your jokes

In suggesting that people keep their jokes within the bounds of good taste, literally "one should employ restraint in his jests," Cicero offered advice that many speakers at public events and private parties would do well to take to heart.

a dicto secundum quid ad dictum simpliciter
aah DIHK-toh seh-KUUN-duum kwihd ahd DIHK-tuum
sihm-PLIH-kih-tehr

from a particular case to a general truth

This characterization criticizes the drawing of broad generalizations from a single valid observation. So if Mary, whose
parents both graduated from Yale, is accepted into the freshman
class, we cannot depend on the fact that *everyone* whose parents graduated from Yale will be accepted.

a dicto simpliciter ad dictum secundum quid
aah DIHK-toh sihm-PLIH-kih-tehr ahd DIHK-tuum seh-
KUUN-duum kwihd

from a general truth to a particular case

This inversion of the preceding observation points out that
we may not properly apply a generalization to a particular case
without considering the possible uniqueness of that case. Even
if most world-famous musicians were once child prodigies, we
should not expect every young child who exhibits exceptional
musical talent to become a world-famous musician.

ad ignorantiam
ahd ihg-noh-RAHN-tih-yahm

to ignorance

In law, an argument in a trial may be based *ad ignorantiam*,
that is, on one's opponent's ignorance of the facts in the case.
Again, a judicial decision may be appealed *ad ignorantiam*, that
is, on the basis that the case was decided without knowledge
of important information that was known but went unrevealed
during the trial.

ad impossibile nemo tenetur
ahd ihm-paws-SIH-bih-leh NAY-moh teh-NAY-tuur

don't be surprised when you don't bat .400

This small wisdom, "nobody is held to the impossible," is designed to prevent heartbreak. While people should strive to do their best, they must not set their hearts on goals that are virtually impossible for them to achieve.

ad initium
ahd ih-NIH-tih-yuum
to *or* at the beginning

See also A PRINCIPIO.

ad instar
ahd EEN-stahr
after the fashion of

This phrase may be used to indicate a literary creation or work of art done in the style of a master. Thus, an oration may be written in the style of a great orator, as **ad instar Ciceronis** (kih-keh-ROH-nihs), "in the manner of Cicero." But *instar* may also be translated as "likeness," giving us the phrase **ad instar omnium** (AWM-nih-yuum), "in the likeness of all," suggesting a lack of individuality. So if we are striving for excellence, we ought to eschew unoriginality.

ad internecionem
ahd ihn-tehr-neh-kih-YOH-nehm
to slaughter

A bloody and completely final phrase that makes a mockery of what we are used to thinking of as civilized behavior. It characterizes warfare in which no quarter is shown to an enemy army. Thus, "a war *ad internecionem*" is a war of extermination, and the noun *internecio*, which may be translated as "massacre" or "extermination," suggests the brutality shown in modern times in the term "Holocaust" or more recently in so-called ethnic cleansing. It is worth pointing out that the English adjective "internecine" most correctly conveys the meaning of "mutually destructive," but in "internecine strife" has taken on the meaning of "a struggle or conflict within a group." While the etymology of the term does not suggest this meaning, we must all be aware that the bitterest—even the most savage—conflicts often occur between members of a family. Consider, for example, the bloody toll of the United States Civil War, aptly characterized as a war between brothers.

ad invidiam
ahd ihn-WIH-dih-yahm

to envy

This phrase is used to characterize an argument or appeal— **argumentum** (ahr-goo-MEHN-tuum) **ad invidiam**—not based on reason or supporting evidence yet powerful in effect and frequently employed by the unscrupulous rabble-rouser, always ready to appeal to envy, jealousy, prejudice, malice, or ill will.

ad iudicium (or judicium)
ahd yoo-DIH-kih-yuum

to common sense

This phrase, literally "to judgment," is used to characterize an argument or appeal, **argumentum** (ahr-goo-MEHN-tuum) **ad iudicium**, based on logic or factual evidence, which can be counted on to convince reasonable people. Or can it?

adiuvante (or adjuvante) Deo labor proficit
ahd-yuu-WAHN-teh DEH-yoh LAH-bawr PROH-fih-kiht

with God's help, work prospers

A humble response to such intrusive questions as "How's business?" and "How's the novel coming?" or even "Do you think you can clean your room by lunchtime?"

ad manum
ahd MAH-nuum

in readiness

A happy phrase, literally "at hand," telling the world, for example, that an assignment, project, or the like is complete. But it can also be used more widely. "The money for this month's rent is *ad manum.*" "She soon became aware that the solution to her problem was not *ad manum.*"

ad meliora vertamur
ahd meh-lih-YOH-rah wehr-TAAH-muur
let's change the subject

A handy expression, literally "let us turn to better things," useful for turning attention away from an embarrassing or depressing subject that is under discussion. (See also SED HAEC HACTENUS.)

ad misericordiam
ahd mih-seh-rih-KAWR-dih-yahm
to pity

When all other arguments fail, one can appeal *ad misericordiam*, hoping that a court or one's opponent will be moved to show sympathy and grant mercy—both "sympathy" and "mercy" are additional translations of *misericordia.*

ad modum
ahd MAW-duum
like

This phrase, also rendered as "after the manner of," provides an opportunity to employ the compressed Latin phrase in place of its lengthier—and more common—English equivalent: "It would not be farfetched to say the young violinist played *ad modum* Heifetz." By adding *hunc* (huunk) to *ad modum*, we get **ad hunc modum**, "like this." A useful locution: "If you carry on *ad hunc modum*, you'll gain nothing."

ad multos annos
ahd MUUL-tohs AHN-nohs
l'chaim

A toast, of course, literally "for many years," and often taken as "long life!" although "to life," as given above in Hebrew, will also do. The more common Latin toast is **prosit** (PROH-siht), "may it benefit you," but it is also translated as any of the three English renderings here given.

ad oculos
ahd AW-kuu-lohs
visibly

Literally "to the eyes."

ad summam
ahd SUUM-mahm
in short

Also translated as "in fact," "in a word," and "in conclusion," *ad summam* is useful especially when the words following it are brief and to the point. *Summam* is a form of the noun **summa** (SUUM-mah), meaning "chief point," "summary," "essence," and other similar terms. *Ad summam* must not be confused with the following entry, AD SUMMUM, employing a form of **summus** (SUUM-muus), meaning "highest."

ad summum
ahd SUUM-muum
to the highest point

Also taken as "to the surface" and "to the top," and the phrase **summum bonum** (SUUM-muum BAW-nuum) means "the highest good." The noun "summit," of course, lurks in the adjective **summus** (SUUM-muus), "highest." (See the previous entry, AD SUMMAM, for a useful clarification.)

ad usum
ahd OO-suum
according to custom

This phrase may also be taken as "according to usage," giving lexicographers as well as social commentators a peg on which to hang their judgmental pronouncements.

adversa virtute repello
ahd-WEHR-sah wihr-TOO-teh reh-PEHL-loh
I repulse adversity by courage (or valor)

Maybe so, but not when I'm confronted by an armed mugger. After all, a sixteenth-century proverb teaches us that discretion is the better part of valor. (See also NOLI IRRITARE LEONES.)

aegroto dum anima est spes esse dicitur
ī-GROH-toh duum AH-nih-mah ehst spays EHS-seh DEE-kih-tuur
where there's life, there's hope

Cicero telling us, more literally, "as long as a sick man has breath, he has hope." Too often, a slender reed to which to cling.

aemulatio vicini
ī-muu-LAAH-tih-yoh wee-KEE-nee
neighborly envy

In law the phrase, literally "the ill will of a neighbor," telling us that it is illegal for a landowner to act maliciously toward an adjacent landowner, for example by intentionally depriving the neighbor's property of a water view.

aequabiliter et diligenter
ī-kwaah-BIH-lih-tehr eht dee-lih-GEHN-tehr
impartially and conscientiously

A welcome phrase, useful in characterizing the actions of an admirable judge, arbiter, or teacher. "She makes decisions *aequabiliter et diligenter*."

aequam memento rebus in arduis servare mentem
Ī-kwahm meh-MEHN-toh RAY-buus ihn AHR-duu-ees sehr-WAAH-reh MEHN-tehm
keep your cool

Horace advises us to "remember to keep an unruffled mind in difficulties." To which those of us who are weak reply, "Easier said than done." (See also SAEVIS TRANQUILLUS IN UNDIS.)

aes alienum
īs ah-lih-YAY-nuum
debt

Any stockbroker should keep in mind that *aes alienum*, while meaning "debt" or "borrowed money," translates literally as "another's money." Something to keep in mind when touting a penny stock or suggesting a risky investment. (See AES SUUM.)

aes suum
īs SUU-wuum
one's own money

Just as it is important for stockbrokers to keep AES ALIENUM (see above) in mind when recommending investments to clients, it is also suggested that the brokers keep *aes suum* in mind. Thus admonished, brokers will treat their clients' money with the same care given to the brokers' own money. A word of caution: Some people acting in a fiduciary role have been known to become too literal in treating their clients' money as their own.

aeternum servans sub pectore vulnus
ī-TEHR-nuum SEHR-waahns suub PEHK-taw-reh WUUL-nuus

bearing a grudge

The human animal has an unsurpassed ability to remember, but does that gift always work to our advantage? Surely it did not avail Juno. In Virgil's *Aeneid*, Juno, "nursing an everlasting wound within her breast," relentlessly and in vain tried to prevent the Trojans from attaining their fated glory. Today, of course, we are too enlightened to nurse grudges for very long.

afflatus
ahf-FLAAH-tuus

inspiration

This term, also given as **adflatus** (ahd-FLAAH-tuus), has as its primary meanings "breath," "breeze," and "wind," suggesting the belief of ancient Romans that a divine source breathed upon the writer or artist to impart inspiration. And "inspiration" itself derives from the Latin verb **inspirare** (een-spee-RAAH-reh), "breathe upon *or* into." For many centuries, of course, "afflatus" (ə-FLAY-təs) has had a place in the English language, with the meaning "inspiration."

afflavit Deus et dissipantur
ahf-FLAAH-wiht DEH-yuus eht dihs-sih-PAHN-tuur

God breathed and they were put to flight

This is one version of the inscription on a medal struck in commemoration of the destruction of the Spanish Armada in 1588. The inscription is also given as **flavit Jehovah et dissipati sunt** (FLAAH-wiht yeh-HOH-wah eht dihs-sih-PAAH-tee suunt), "Jehovah breathed and they were dispersed." You might think that Sir Frances Drake and the English fleet had something to do with the victory, but it is recorded that mighty storms at sea during the period of the battle were of great assistance in destroying the Spanish fleet. So there is some credence for the divine intervention suggested by both versions of the inscription on the medal. Note that neither inscription said anything about Drake or his cohorts. Whether you accept the idea of divine intervention is for you to decide.

a fonte puro pura defluit aqua
aah FAWN-teh POO-roh POO-rah DAY-fluu-wiht AH-kwah
from a pure spring flows pure water

A thought whose verity extends far beyond water sources. For example, it could be used to characterize the content of a sermon preached by a favorite minister, or to describe the thoughts expressed by an innocent child.

agenti incumbit probatio
ah-GEHN-tee ihn-KUUM-biht praw-BAAH-tih-yoh
the burden of proof falls on the one bringing the suit

A principle established in Roman law and still followed widely today. It has the effect in a criminal trial, for example, of obliging the prosecutor to present evidence that the court or jury could reasonably believe in support of the contention that the accused person is guilty as charged, failing which the case will be lost. *Agenti incumbit probatio* defines the so-called burden of proof, in Latin **onus probandi** (AW-nuus praw-BAHN-dee), literally "the burden of proving." In civil cases, the burden of proof falls on the attorney for the person who has made the charge and seeks redress.

alea belli incerti
AAH-leh-yah BEHL-lee ihn-KEHR-tee
you never know how a war will turn out

This insight, literally "the hazard of an uncertain war," has given rise to a profession whose function is to predict the chances of success or failure in a contemplated military venture. These analysts are employed by governments and think tanks, and we read their articles in learned journals, buy their books, and watch many of them pontificating on the media. Notice that

Caesar's portentous remark **alea iacta est** (AAH-leh-yah YAHK-tah ehst), commonly expressed as "the die is cast," refers to the game of dice, which supports the notion that launching a war is always a gamble.

aliam excute quercum
AH-lih-yahm EHKS-kuu-teh KWEHR-kuum
get lost!

A colorful Latin phrase to use in turning down a proposition or denying a request for a favor, usually a loan. The response *aliam excute quercum,* literally "shake out some other oak," tells the person to whom it is addressed that he or she is barking up the wrong tree and should look elsewhere.

alia tendanda via est
AH-lih-yah tehn-DAHN-dah WIH-yah ehst
go back to the drawing board

More literally "another way must be tried," suggesting strongly that someone's present efforts will prove fruitless.

aliena optimum frui insania
AH-lih-YAY-naah AWP-tih-muum FRUU-wee een-SAAH-nih-yaah
learn from the mistakes of others

The intent of this observation, more literally "it's a very good thing to enjoy the folly of others," is to encourage us not to repeat mistakes made by other people. Too often, such advice falls on deaf ears and we are doomed to repeat past errors.

alienatus a se
ah-lih-yay-NAAH-tuus aah say
out of character

An apt description of one afflicted with a personality-altering psychological disorder, literally "estranged from oneself."

aliena vitia in oculis habemus, a tergo nostra sunt
ah-lih-YAY-nah WIH-tih-yah ihn AW-kuu-lees hah-BAY-
muus aah TEHR-goh NAWS-trah suunt

> Oh wad some power the giftie gie us
> To see oursels as others see us!

In these lines Robert Burns told us that while we are quick to recognize shortcomings of character in other people, we are blind to our own. Seneca the Younger expressed the same thought in *aliena vitia in oculis habemus, a tergo nostra sunt,* literally "another's faults are before our eyes, our own are behind us." (See also ALIQUIS NON DEBET ESSE IUDEX IN PROPRIA CAUSA.)

alieni appetens
ah-lih-YAY-nee AHP-peh-tayns

covetous

This phrase, literally "greedy for another's property," describes covetousness, second among the seven deadly sins and tenth among the Ten Commandments. *Alieni appetens* also is part of a larger phrase, **alieni appetens, sui profusus** (SUU-wee praw-FOO-suus). This larger phrase has the literal meaning "covetous for another's property, wasteful of his own." Sallust, a first-century B.C. Roman historian, used it to characterize Catiline, the Roman nobleman whose conspiratorial activities made him a target of Cicero and Cicero's supporters. Since human failings have not changed all that much since the first century B.C., we can still find use for *alieni appetens, sui profusus.* (See also QUOUSQUE TANDEM ABUTERE PATIENTIA NOSTRA?)

alio intuitu
AH-lih-yoh ihn-TUU-wih-too

from another point of view

When the search for a solution to a vexing problem hits a snag, the thing to do is seek out someone with a fresh mind to review the problem *alio intuitu.* It is surprising how often such a review will quickly yield worthwhile suggestions. Incidentally, *intuitu* is a participial form of the verb **intueri** (ihn-too-WAY-ree), "gaze at" or "contemplate." Which leads one to think that the phenomenon we call "intuition" is not as mysterious as commonly thought—a little contemplation can give us a fresh point of view.

aliquis in omnibus, nullus in singulis
AH-lih-kwihs ihn AWM-nih-buus NOOL-luus ihn SIHN-guu-lees
jack-of-all-trades, master of none

A phrase, more literally "a somebody in general, a nobody in particular," used to describe a generalist rather than an expert in a given area, for example a dilettante as opposed to an artisan.

aliquis non debet esse iudex (or judex) in propria causa
AH-lih-kwihs nohn DAY-beht EHS-seh YOO-dehks ihn PRAW-prih-yaah KOW-saah
how can we be objective in judging ourselves?

This Latin maxim, "nobody should be a judge in his own case," makes it clear that we cannot be trusted to evaluate ourselves or our own work. Wise judges, expert editors, even qualified art or drama or music critics can be counted on for greater objectivity—within the limits of their ability, that is. (See also ALIENA VITIA IN OCULIS HABEMUS, A TERGO NOSTRA SUNT.)

alitur vitium vivitque tegendo
AH-lih-tuur WIH-tih-yuum wee-WIHT-kweh teh-GEHN-doh
whatever you do, don't stonewall

In this small example of wisdom, or at least common sense—literally "a fault is nourished and lives by being concealed"—Virgil urges us not to give in to the human tendency to hide things that should—and inevitably will—become public knowledge despite our best efforts to prevent disclosure. Yet, too many times, the occupant of the Oval Office or other people in powerful and influential positions ignore Virgil's advice and attempt to conceal information from the press and the public. Of course, despite their best efforts, a plethora of troublesome facts inevitably comes to light. When will they ever learn?

aliud corde premunt, aliud ore promunt
AH-lih-yuud KAWR-deh PREH-muunt AH-lih-yuud OH-reh PROH-muunt
no use trying to prevent leaks

Everyone knows that almost no one can keep a secret. *Aliud corde premunt, aliud ore promunt* doesn't explain why. All it tells us is that people are blabbermouths, literally "one thing they conceal in the heart, they disclose another with the mouth." If this has been going on since Roman times at least, why should we be surprised when we read people's most important secrets on the front page of the morning newspaper? (See also ALIUD EST CELARE, ALIUD TACERE.)

aliud est celare, aliud tacere
AH-lih-yuud ehst kay-LAAH-reh AH-lih-yuud tah-KAY-reh
better to play dumb—or is it?

A warning for anyone with something to hide, "it's one thing to conceal, another to be silent." Thus, if someone feels constrained to prevent exposure of certain knowledge—for whatever reason—this admonition tells us that silence may be a better option than inventing a lie to cover up one's own guilt or the guilt of trusted allies. Neither path is that of the virtuous person, who knows better than to become involved in nefarious intrigues. In short, don't ever say or do anything you would hate to become public knowledge. (See also ALITUR VITIUM VIVITQUE TEGENDO, which does not condone concealment.)

aliud et idem
AH-lih-yuud eht ih-dehm
another thing and yet the same

We might say this of the latest work of second-rate playwrights, movie directors, and novelists who regularly clone their earlier efforts. This is also true of movies and TV programs. If they prove successful, they are immediately copied by others or "sequeled" to death.

alium silere quod voles primus sile
AH-lih-yuum sih-LAY-reh kwawd WAW-lays PREE-muus SIH-lay
the surefire way to keep a secret

Advice from Seneca, the poet, philosopher, and counselor to Emperor Nero, "if you want to keep something secret, first say nothing yourself." (For why you must not entrust a secret to others, see ALIUD CORDE PREMUNT, ALIUD ORE PROMUNT.)

allegans contraria non est audiendus
ahl-LAY-gaahns kawn-TRAAH-rih-yah nohn ehst ow-dih-YEHN-duus
close your ears

Literally "he who alleges contradictory things is not to be listened to." How can you trust a person who speaks out of both sides of his mouth?

alma natura
AHL-mah naah-TOO-rah
fostering nature

Just as we enjoy giving universities the glorious appellation **alma mater** (MAAH-tehr), "fostering mother," in *alma natura* we infuse nature with its own golden glow. At the same time we overlook the ravages of time, the devastating impact of tsunamis, earthquakes, hurricanes, and other violent acts of nature, and the occasional volcanic eruption. Fostering nature indeed!

alter ipse amicus
AHL-tehr IHP-seh ah-MEE-kuus
a friend is a second self

The Romans made much of friendship. (For example, see also AMICUS EST TANQUAM ALTER IDEM.)

alteri sic tibi
AHL-teh-ree seek TIH-bih
do unto others

The opening words of the golden rule; in full: "Do unto others as you would have them do unto you." Here, literally, "to another thus to yourself."

altum mare
AHL-tuum MAH-reh
the high sea

A term in law designating the area of a sea or ocean that lies beyond the territorial waters of a country, and thus beyond the jurisdiction of that country.

amabilis insania
ah-MAAH-bih-lihs een-SAAH-nih-yah
lovable folly

A phrase of Ovid also translated as "lovable madness," since *insania* can also be taken as "madness" and as "poetic rapture." Enough said. (See also AMANS IRATUS MULTA MENTITUR SIBI.)

a maiori (or majori) ad minus
aah mah-YOH-ree ahd MIH-nuus
leading from strength

Said of a form of argument or proof, literally "from the greater to the less," that presents the most telling evidence first and then goes down the line to the least important. Arguing *a maiori ad minus* will at least make sure that in a trial one's best points are presented to a jury before any of the jurors nod off.

amans iratus multa mentitur sibi

AH-maahns ee-RAAH-tuus MUUL-tah MEHN-tih-tuur SIH-bih

an angry lover tells himself many lies

Publilius Syrus, who well understood human nature, telling us not to trust the judgment of a spurned lover. (See also AMABILIS INSANIA and AMARE ET SAPERE VIX DEO CONCEDITUR.)

amare et sapere vix deo conceditur

ah-MAAH-reh eht SAH-peh-reh wihks DEH-yoh kawn-KAY-dih-tuur

crazy in love

Publilius Syrus, again demonstrating profound knowledge of human nature, gives us this maxim, "to love and be wise is scarcely granted even to a god." No wonder we say "mad about you." (See also AMABILIS INSANIA and AMANS IRATUS MULTA MENTITUR SIBI.)

amari aliquid

ah-MAAH-ree AH-lih-kwihd

a touch of bitterness

We can all be certain that sometime in our lives, and sooner rather than later, we will experience *amari aliquid*, literally "something bitter."

a mari usque ad mare

aah MAH-ree OOS-kweh ahd MAH-reh

from sea to sea

The motto of the Dominion of Canada, more literally "from the sea all the way to the sea." In "America the Beautiful," we sing of brotherhood "from sea to shining sea." In the case of Canada and the United States, of course, the seas are in fact oceans. But who can make a strong rhyme employing "from ocean to ocean"? Again, while the Romans had the word **oceanus** (oh-

KEH-yah-nuus), which they borrowed from the Greek *okeanos*, in Homer considered to be a river that surrounded the earth, they used *mare* more often to mean "ocean." Really now, who knew from real oceans back in ancient Rome or in Homer's time?

ambigendi locus
ahm-bih-GEHN-dee LAW-kuus
room for doubt

amici fures temporis
ah-MEE-kee FOO-rays TEHM-paw-rihs
friends are thieves of time

As much as the Romans valued friendship, they knew it was a mistake to give oneself freely to friends when serious work was lying undone. And if they had invented telephones, cell phones, and computers, they would surely have used answering machines, text messaging, and e-mail. (See also DUM LOQUOR, HORA FUGIT.)

amici probantur rebus adversis
ah-MEE-kee praw-BAHN-tuur RAY-buus ahd-WEHR-sees
the friendship litmus test

Seneca the Younger, in "friends are proved by adversity," telling us how to distinguish true friends from fair-weather friends. (See also AMICUS CERTUS IN RE INCERTA CERNITUR.)

amicitia semper prodest
ah-mee-KIH-tih-yah SEHM-pehr PROH-dehst
don't forget your friends

Here's Seneca the Younger again on friendship, this time telling us that "friendship is always of benefit." (See also AMICI PROBANTUR REBUS ADVERSIS.)

amicus certus in re incerta cernitur
ah-MEE-kuus KEHR-tuus ihn ray ihn-KEHR-taah KEHR-nih-tuur
when things get iffy, you find out who your true friends are

Here is Cicero, quoting the second-century B.C. Roman poet Quintus Ennius on the true test of friendship, telling us literally that "a reliable friend is discerned in an uncertain affair." We are more apt to say "a friend in need is a friend indeed," a locution with roots in the Latin *amicus certus in re incerta cernitur.* (For Seneca's version of this thought, see AMICI PROBANTUR REBUS ADVERSIS.)

amicus est tanquam alter idem
ah-MEE-kuus ehst TAHN-kwahm AHL-tehr EE-dehm
a friend is just like a second self

For us such a claim applies only to a close friend, but the Romans didn't throw the term *amicus* around. For them, every friend was a close friend. (See also ALTER IPSE AMICUS.)

amissum quod nescitur non amittitur
aah-MEES-suum kwawd NAYS-kih-tuur nohn aah-MIHT-tih-tuur
what you don't know won't hurt you

This maxim of Publilius Syrus, "a loss that is unknown is no loss at all," offers a valuable insight that can be applied to a variety of life's travails.

amor gignit amorem
AH-mawr GIHG-niht ah-MOH-rehm
love begets love

So they say. At least it's worth trying. (See also SI VIS AMARI AMA.)

amor habendi
AH-mawr hah-BEHN-dee
love of possessing

A dangerous proclivity, more vividly identified by Ovid as **amor sceleratus** (skeh-leh-RAAH-tuus, "accursed") **habendi**, giving us "the accursed love of possessing." Ovid clearly was thinking of the many people who carry possessing to an extreme.

amor tussisque non celantur
AH-mawr tuus-SIHS-kweh nohn keh-LAHN-tuur
love and a cough cannot be hidden

See also NEC AMOR NEC TUSSIS CELATUR.

aniles fabulae
ah-NEE-lays FAAH-buu-lī
old wives' tales

Be careful before you dismiss one as such.

animal disputans
AH-nih-mahl DIHS-puu-taahns
an ornery critter

An apt characterization of a curmudgeon, literally "a disputatious creature," who automatically takes exception to anyone and anything, who casts doubt on the efficacy of every proposed idea, and who hates every new book, movie, or video game—in short, not the sort of person you'd want to have a beer with.

animal rationale
AH-nih-mahl rah-tih-yoh-NAAH-leh
the human animal

In this self-adulatory term, literally "the reasoning animal," we humans proudly call attention to our ability to reason, which is said to differentiate us from so-called lower animals. Of course, we periodically go to war with the intention of destroying as many other people as we can and continually do our best to exhaust our natural resources—proving beyond any doubt that we are indeed reasoning animals.

animo et fide
AH-nih-moh eht FIH-deh
by courage and faith

A motto positing that with courage and faith a family or other form of social organization will inevitably manage to succeed. Or muddle through?

animo non astutia
AH-nih-moh nohn ahs-TOO-tih-yaah
by courage, not by cunning

Another splendid motto for those who see themselves as brave and virtuous. How admirable are our qualities, at least in our own eyes. (See also ANIMO ET FIDE.)

animus furandi
AH-nih-muus foo-RAHN-dee
the intention of stealing

A legal phrase defining the mind-set of a person found guilty of stealing. "He said he acted on impulse, but clearly he broke into the house with *animus furandi*."

animus meminisse horret
AH-nih-muus meh-mih-NIHS-seh HAWR-reht
I can't bear to think of it

A locution from Virgil, literally "my soul shudders to remember," useful for anyone who has had terrible experiences and prefers not to talk about them—or, more often, for one who is about to launch into a gruesome description of past experiences.

anni nubiles

AHN-nee NOO-bih-lays

age of consent

The Latin phrase, literally "marriageable years," defining the age at which a person becomes legally competent to consent to marriage or to sexual intercourse.

ante lucem

AHN-teh LOO-kehm

just before daybreak

Literally "before light," the moments *ante lucem* precede "first light" or "dawn," in Latin **aurora** (ow-ROH-rah).

ante tubam trepidat

AHN-teh TUU-bahm TREH-pih-daht

he's wounded before a shot is fired

Anyone who has had firsthand knowledge of fear in battle knows it is not uncommon to begin to shake—or worse—even before the first gun is fired. In Roman times, the sounding of a battle trumpet signaled the start of serious business. *Ante tubam trepidat*, thus, suggests a soldier who becomes frightened before a battle begins, literally "he is alarmed before the trumpet [sounds]."

ante victoriam ne canas triumphum

AHN-teh wihk-TOH-rih-yahm nay KAH-naahs trih-YUUM-phuum

don't count your chickens before they're hatched

Very good advice for finalists in a tennis match; there's many a slip between Davis Cup and lip. Or, as Roman realists knew, when they said "do not sing your triumph before the victory." And let's all recall the wise words attributed to Yogi Berra, "It ain't over till it's over."

antiqua homo virtute ac fide
ahn-TEE-kwaah HAW-moh wihr-TOO-teh ahk FIH-deh
they don't make them like that no more

Terence characterizing a person of estimable character as "a man of the old-time virtue and good faith." We might describe this person as "from the old school."

a posse ad esse
aah PAWS-seh ahd EHS-seh
from possibility to actuality

A good motto for a firm of architects who provide service from initial drawings through completed structure, who might say, "We see our projects through *a posse ad esse.*" On the other hand, the clients of the firm might one day say, "The entire procedure was a mess *a posse ad esse.*"

apparatus belli
ahp-pah-RAAH-tuus BEHL-lee
the apparatus of war

This term includes everything needed for war, from uniforms to food to guns to ammunition to all the rest.

apparent rari nantes in gurgite vasto
ahp-PAAH-rehnt RAAH-ree NAHN-tays ihn GUUR-gih-teh WAHS-toh
scattered swimmers appear in the vast whirlpool

Virgil's description of the few struggling survivors of a storm at sea can be used to describe a poor literary work offering a few worthwhile thoughts but obscuring them in an ocean of unnecessary words. A gem or two buried in a pile of manure.

a principio
aah preen-KIH-pih-yoh
from the beginning

> See also AD INITIUM.

aquilam volare doces
AH-kwih-lahm waw-LAAH-reh DAW-kays
you're teaching an eagle to fly

> We are being told not to do what does not have to be done. Anyone who has seen an eagle on the wing knows it needs no flight training. (See also DELPHINUM NATARE DOCES.)

aquila non capit muscas
AH-kwih-lah nohn KAH-piht MUUS-kaahs
I'm too important to bother with small fry

> Anyone—or any nation—with an inflated self-concept may turn aside interruptions—or threats—with this locution, "an eagle doesn't catch flies." Bullies, on the other hand, spend all their time catching flies. And great nations periodically flex their muscles at the expense of tiny nations.

arcana imperii
ahr-KAAH-nah ihm-PEH-rih-yee
state secrets

> This phrase translates literally as "the secrets (or mysteries) of empire (or government)." Unfortunately, it is the habit of governments to classify nearly everything as secret.

ardentia verba
ahr-DEHN-tih-yah WEHR-bah
glowing language

More literally "burning words," but however *ardentia verba* is translated, you can be sure you'll recognize and appreciate such words when you encounter them.

arenae mandas semina
ah-RAY-nī MAHN-daahs SAY-mih-nah
you're attempting the impossible

Any farmer knows better than to try to raise a crop in sand. *Arenae mandas semina*, literally "you're entrusting seeds to sand," tells all of us not to waste our energy on vain enterprises. (See also ARENA SINE CALCE and EX ARENA FUNICULUM NECTIS.)

arena sine calce
ah-RAY-nah SIH-neh KAHL-keh
sand without lime

A line of reasoning that does not hold together may be described as *arena sine calce*. The metaphor, used by Suetonius to characterize loose statements that have nothing to bind them together, alludes to the impossibility of creating a stable mixture of sand and water without lime or some other material that enables sand to hold together. (See also EX ARENA FUNICULUM NECTIS.)

argumenti causa
ahr-goo-MEHN-tee KOW-saah
for the sake of argument

Also given as **argumenti gratia** (GRAAH-tih-yaah), with the same meaning—and don't you hate people who habitually argue *argumenti causa*?

arma in armatos sumere iura (or jura) sinunt
AHR-mah ihn ahr-MAAH-tohs SOO-meh-reh YOO-rah SIH-nuunt
it's OK to shoot someone who's pointing a gun at you

Nations appear to need no excuse for making war, but here is one anyway, "the laws permit the taking up of arms against those (who are) armed." This precept has long been followed to an extreme by nations—and individuals—who undertake so-called preemptive strikes in the face of a perceived, often imaginary, threat.

arma pacis fulcra
AHR-mah PAAH-kihs FUUL-krah

arms are the props of peace

It is easy to see why the Romans took this maxim to heart. After all, at the height of their power they had to manage an enormous empire and thus were always in danger of attack on their borders as well as having to remain alert in the face of possible internal threats. (See also ARMA TUENTUR PACEM.)

arma tuentur pacem
AHR-mah tuu-WEHN-tuur PAAH-kehm

arms guard peace

Another plug for the importance of maintaining strong military forces. Despite—because of?—the ever-increasing output and sale of guns in our century, armed hostilities are proliferating almost everywhere, leading one to wonder whether "arms guard peace" is an example of Orwellian doublespeak. (See also ARMA PACIS FULCRA.)

asinus ad lyram
AH-sih-nuus ahd LÜ-rahm

an ass at the lyre

A strong characterization applied to anyone totally devoid of appreciation or talent for anything artistic; for example, in music someone with a tin ear, in art someone with no eye for beauty.

asinus asino, et sus sui pulcher
AH-sih-nuus AH-sih-noh eht soos SUU-wee PUUL-khehr
there's someone for everybody

This observation, "an ass is beautiful to an ass, and a pig to a pig," may not appear to be a felicitous way of alluding to people and the way they appear to one another, but it is comforting to believe that beauty may really be in the eye of the beholder.

a teneris annis
aah TEH-neh-rees AHN-nees
from tender years

at spes non fracta
aht spays nohn FRAAHK-tah
you can't keep a good man (or woman) down

An apt phrase, literally "but hope is not shattered," for those who go on courageously and relentlessly in the face of extreme hardship. And there are such people. Consider this stanza from the poem "Invictus" (Latin, ihn-WEEK-tuus; English, in-VIK-təs, "unbeaten") by the nineteenth-century English poet William Ernest Henley:

> In the fell clutch of circumstance,
> I have not winced nor cried aloud;
> Under the bludgeonings of chance
> My head is bloody, but unbowed.

(See also INVICTUS MANEO.)

auctor pretiosa facit
OWK-tawr preh-tih-YOH-sah FAH-kiht
the giver makes (the gifts) precious

For a fuller form of this saccharine observation, see ACCEPTIS-SIMA SEMPER MUNERA SUNT AUCTOR QUAE PRETIOSA FACIT.

audacia pro muro habetur

ow-DAAH-kih-yah proh MOO-roh hah-BAY-tuur

there's nothing like a brave front

Anyone or any nation faced with an imminent threat knows that there are three ways to respond: Look tough and ready for combat yourself, fall on your knees and beg for mercy, or be brave and willing to compromise. In this maxim, literally "audacity serves as a defense," from Sallust, a first-century B.C. Roman historian, we are advised to adopt the first stance—"I am ready for you, and you will pay a price for any act of aggression you undertake."

audacter calumniare semper aliquid haeret

ow-DAAHK-tehr kah-luum-nih-YAAH-reh SEHM-pehr AH-lih-kwihd HĪ-reht

talk about negative campaigning!

This advice, "slander boldly, something always sticks," goes way back in time—and, for the slanderer, has more often than not been proved effective. So while our century has had its share of shameless lying, we certainly didn't invent the technique. (See also AUDACTER TE VENDITA SEMPER ALIQUID HAERET.)

audacter et sincere

ow-DAAHK-tehr eht sihn-KAY-ray

boldly and frankly

A good motto to emblazon on a coat of arms. But not always a way to make friends and influence people.

audacter te vendita semper aliquid haeret

ow-DAAHK-tehr tay WAYN-dih-taah SEHM-pehr AH-lih-kwihd HĪ-reht

if you don't blow your own horn, who will?

Advice, "praise yourself boldly, something always sticks," that frequently is advanced by egotistical superstars. (See also AUDACTER CALUMNIARE SEMPER ALIQUID HAERET.)

audax et cautus
OW-daahks eht KOW-tuus
bold and wary

A motto incorporating the idea that one ought to move ahead fearlessly, but with a dash of caution. (See also AUDE SAPERE.)

aude sapere
OW-day SAH-peh-reh
dare to be wise

Also translated as "dare to think independently." It takes strength of character to think outside the box, for example, to spurn well-intentioned advice from parents and less than well-intentioned advice from imprudent friends. Also given as SAPERE AUDE.

audi vide tace si vis vivere in pace
OW-dee WIH-day TAH-kay see wees WEE-weh-reh ihn PAAH-keh
hear no evil, see no evil, speak no evil

The wise person knows that there are times when one must speak up and times when it is better to keep one's own counsel. The advice given in this proverb, "hear, see, be silent if you wish to live in peace," teaches us the safe way—yet not always the most honorable way—to conduct ourselves. What this proverb does not tell us is how to know when to talk and when not to talk.

auribus teneo lupum
OW-rih-buus TEH-neh-yoh LUU-puum
I've got a tiger by the tail

Anyone facing a problem for which there is no good solution may say *auribus teneo lupum,* "I'm holding a wolf by the ears." Thus, I cannot hold on forever, and I cannot let go—either action will leave me at the mercy of the beast. As the wise reader knows, the way out of this dilemma is to avoid getting into it.

aut amat aut odit mulier nihil est tertium
owt AH-maht owt OH-diht MUU-lih-yehr NIH-hihl ehst TEHR-tih-yuum

why can't they just be friends?

Talk about stereotypes! This is one of those marvelous insights—"a woman either loves or hates, there is no third way"—that must have endeared the men of ancient Rome to women, and it is still bothering women today.

aut mors aut victoria
owt mawrs owt week-TOH-rih-yah

either death or victory

Like many of today's coaches—whose employment depends more on the ability to produce victories than to foster ethical behavior on the playing field—Roman generals weren't kidding when they sent their troops out to do battle. This stirring battle cry is also given as **aut vincere aut mori** (owt WIHN-keh-reh owt MAW-ree), "either to conquer or to die." (See also VINCERE AUT MORI.)

aut non tentaris aut perfice
owt nohn tehn-TAAH-rihs owt PEHR-fih-keh

don't start anything you can't finish

This advice from Ovid, literally "either don't attempt it or else finish it," is intended to teach us good work habits. But while we should not habitually leave things half done, isn't it better to abandon an idea that shows sure signs of eventual failure than to carry it through to the bitter end?

aut prodesse volunt aut delectare poetae

owt proh-DEHS-seh WAW-luunt owt day-lehk-TAAH-reh
paw-WAY-tī

poets want either to profit or to please

Horace made this interesting observation in his epistolary
poem *Ars Poetica* (ahrs paw-WAY-tih-kah, "The Art of Poetry").
Good to know that poets had both feet on the ground way back
in the first century B.C.

aut vitam aut culpam

owt WEE-tahm owt KUUL-pahm

just behave yourself

When someone is given a so-called lifetime appointment—
usually to a high judicial post—the appointment is not intended
to be entirely unconditional. Thus, the phrase *aut vitam aut
culpam,* literally "for life or until misconduct," may be made part
of the official notice of appointment.

auxilium ab alto

owks-IH-lih-yuum ahb AHL-toh

help from on high

Sometimes it may seem that a little
divine intervention is our only hope for
extricating ourselves from the mess we
are in.

a verbis ad verbera

aah WEHR-bees ahd WEHR-beh-rah

one thing leads to another

When a friendly discussion leads to strong disagreement and
finally to fisticuffs, it has gone *a verbis ad verbera,* literally "from
words to blows."

B

barbae tenus sapientes

BAHR-bī TEH-nuus sah-pih-YEHN-tays

know-it-alls

Literally "men wise as far as a beard (makes them appear wise)." This saying refers to people with inflated egos (and conspicuous beards) who pretend to knowledge they do not have. *Barbae tenus sapientes*, which evokes the image of young men who affect beards to make them look older and wiser, gives us a welcome phrase for referring to such men.

basis virtutum constantia

BAH-sihs wihr-TOO-tuum kohn-STAHN-tih-yah

just keep at it

Forget about Mozart, John Stuart Mill, and all the other famous child prodigies. If you're old enough to read this book, you're already too old to make it big in childhood. So what to do? *Basis virtutum constantia*, literally "steadiness is the pedestal of excellence," gives us the clue: Never stop trying to achieve whatever it is you really want to achieve.

beatus ille qui procul negotiis

beh-YAAH-tuus IHL-leh kwee PRAW-kuul neh-GOH-tih-yees

move to Vermont

Horace praising the joys of leisure, "happy the man who lives far away from the cares of business." And that goes for women, too. For a paraphrase of Horace referring to a working woman, substitute **beata illa quae** (beh-YAAH-tah IHL-lah kwī) **procul negotiis**.

bellum internecinum
BEHL-luum ihn-tehr-neh-KEE-nuum
a murderous war

More usually called "a war of extermination." For more on this distasteful subject, see AD INTERNECIONEM.

bellum letale
BEHL-luum lay-TAAH-leh
a deadly war

bellum nec timendum nec provocandum
BEHL-luum nehk tih-MEHN-duum nehk proh-waw-KAHN-duum
don't run from or invite war

A Roman view of war, literally "war is neither to be feared nor to be provoked," that suggests a gung-ho mindset combined with enough good sense to make war seem almost acceptable. But doesn't it smack of advice that might be given by the too-old-to-be-drafted to the too-young-to-vote? (See also DULCE BELLUM INEXPERTIS.)

bellum omnium in omnes
BEHL-luum AWM-nih-yuum ihn AWM-nays
run for the hills

Talk about war! *Bellum omnium in omnes* is the big one, literally "the war of all against all."

belua multorum capitum
BAY-luu-wah muul-TOH-ruum KAH-pih-tuum
the multitude

Horace, in a far from democratic moment, denigrating the vast number of ordinary people by calling them "the monster of many heads."

bene decessit
BEH-neh day-KEHS-siht
the way to go

When someone has died a natural death or has died under honorable circumstances, we may say of him or her, *bene decessit,* "he (or she) has died well."

bene est tentare
BEH-neh ehst tehn-TAAH-reh
there's nothing to lose

When your cause is just and you have some chance of achieving success, follow this advice, literally "it is as well to try."

bene exeat
BEH-neh EHKS-eh-yaht
a good character reference

This phrase, "let him (or her) go forth well," is the Roman equivalent of a personal or institutional letter of recommendation.

beneficium invito non datur
beh-neh-FIH-kih-yuum ihn-WEE-toh nohn DAH-tuur
I thought it was just a gift

This maxim, literally "a benefit cannot be bestowed on an unwilling person," advises us to question whether an exceptional act of generosity carries with it an unstated expectation that something—perhaps something illicit—is expected in return, that is, **quid pro quo** (kwihd proh kwoh), literally "something for something."

bene merenti
BEH-neh meh-REHN-tee
to the well-deserving

A phrase that may be used when bestowing a gift or award: "Today we are gathered to pay homage to our retiring leader *bene merenti.*" The plural is **bene merentibus** (meh-REHN-tih-buus).

bene meritus
BEH-neh MEH-rih-tuus
having well deserved

An alternative form of BENE MERENTI. The feminine form is **bene merita** (MEH-rih-tah) and the plural is **bene meriti** (MEH-rih-tee).

bene nati, bene vestiti, et mediocriter docti
BEH-neh NAAH-tee BEH-neh wehs-TEE-tee eht meh-dih-YAW-krih-tehr DAWK-tee
don't judge a book by its cover

Literally, "well born, well dressed, and so-so in learning." Know anyone who fits this description? (See also NE FRONTI CREDE.)

bene qui coniecit (or conjecit) vatem hunc perhibebo optimum
BEH-neh kwee kawn-YAY-kiht WAAH-tehm huunk pehr-hih-BAY-boh AWP-tih-muum
watch out for economists, racetrack touts, and meteorologists

Cicero offering us cynical and wise words on those who make their livings by predicting future events, literally "I shall always assert that he who guessed well was the best prophet."

bene qui latuit bene vixit
BEH-neh kwee LAH-tuu-wiht BEH-neh WEEKS-iht
avoid the limelight

Ovid telling us that if we want happiness, we should not pursue fame, more literally "well has he lived who has lived in obscurity."

benigno numine
beh-NIHG-noh NOO-mih-neh
with a favoring providence

Horace has given us a self-effacing way of explaining whatever success we manage to achieve: "I made it to where I am *benigno numine.*" The phrase may also serve as a modest way of requesting divine assistance: "*Benigno numine*, we shall succeed in our search."

bibere venenum in auro
BIH-beh-reh weh-NAY-nuum ihn OW-roh
it's a mistake to flaunt your wealth

This intriguing phrase, "to drink poison from a golden cup," suggests that in Roman times the rich—those who drank from golden cups—were the likely targets of poisoners and other felons. Why would anyone bother to do in the poor, who drank from cups of clay? Who would profit from poisoning a poor person?

bis
bihs
twice

Also translated as "a second time" or "repeat." We also know "bis" as a Latin term taken into Italian and then adopted in English as the equivalent of "encore!" And, of course, some medicine must be taken b.i.d., an abbreviation for **bis in die** (ihn DIH-yay), or twice a day.

bis peccare in bello non licet
bihs pehk-KAAH-reh ihn BEHL-loh nohn LIH-keht
you're allowed one and only one mistake

While many of us may believe that wars are won by strokes of strategic and tactical brilliance, it is more likely that wars are won by the side that makes fewer strategic and tactical blunders. The military maxim given here, literally "to make a mistake twice in war is not allowable," recognizes the validity of this assertion. One mistake? Probably not decisive. But two? Don't ask.

bis pueri senes
bihs PUU-weh-ree SEH-nays
second childhood

This disagreeable observation, literally "old men are children twice," describes the condition known as senility. The same thought also appears in the singular form, **senex bis puer** (SEH-nehks bihs PUU-wehr, "an old man is twice a boy"). Whether plural or singular, let's hope the geneticists and gerontologists one day soon will do something marvelous to prevent or reverse the unhappy condition.

bis vincit qui se vincit in victoria
bihs WIHN-kiht kwee say WIHN-kiht ihn week-TOH-rih-yaah
don't crow

Publilius Syrus giving us sound advice, "he conquers twice who conquers himself in the hour of victory." First of all, nobody—least of all a runner-up—likes boasters. Secondly, so cyclical is the nature of human experience that today's defeated person or nation can be counted on to become tomorrow's winner.

blandae mendacia linguae
BLAHN-dī mehn-DAAH-kih-yah LIHN-gwī
lies of a flattering tongue

Two hundred years ago, Jonathan Swift called flattery "the food of fools." Thus, whereas we all know "flattery will get you nowhere" as a rejoinder to the blandishments of a person striving to gain some favor, we also know that flattery is wonderfully effective. Witness the ironic "flattery will get you everything." All we can hope for is that *blandae mendacia linguae* will alert you and me to be on guard next time we are exposed to flattery.

bona opinio hominum tutior pecunia est

BAW-nah aw-PEE-nih-yoh HAW-mih-nuum TOO-tih-yawr peh-KOO-nih-yaah ehst

guard your reputation as your life

Publilius Syrus telling us how valuable are our reputations, literally "the good opinion of people is safer than money." We've been given this advice many times over the centuries. For example, Shakespeare, in *Othello*, had Iago say, "But he that filches from me my good name . . . makes me poor indeed." This lesson, alas, is not absorbed by all our political leaders until after they have seriously damaged their reputations, and one scandal seems only to lead to the next. Will we ever learn?

boni principii finis bonus

BAW-nee preen-KIH-pih-yee FEE-nihs BAW-nuus

start off on the right foot

Literally "from a good beginning a good ending." A fourteenth-century English proverb conveys the same message, generally given as "a good beginning makes a good ending." In short, everyone knows this observation is valid. The clear implication is, however, that when we start off on the wrong foot, everything can be counted on to go wrong.

bonis nocet quisquis pepercerit malis

BAW-nees NAW-keht KWIHS-kwihs peh-PEHR-keh-riht MAH-lees

stop coddling criminals

People who seek support for harsh judicial systems will welcome this proverb from Publilius Syrus on the question of public safety, literally "whoever spares the wicked harms the good." This is the kind of stuff that leads to the sentencing practice called "three strikes and you're out." Which means "three major criminal convictions and you're in—for life." (See also QUI PARCIT NOCENTIBUS INNOCENTES PUNIT.)

bonis quod bene fit haud perit
BAW-nees kwawd BEH-neh fiht howd PEH-riht
whatever is done for good men is never lost

An observation of Plautus, assuring us that we will always be remembered for our acts of kindness.

bonum commune
BAW-nuum kawm-MOO-neh
the common good

bonus dux bonum reddit militem
BAW-nuus duuks BAW-nuum REHD-diht MEE-lih-tehm
a good leader makes a good soldier

bonus vir semper tiro
BAW-nuus wihr SEHM-pehr TEE-roh
always willing to learn

This maxim, "a good man is always a beginner," teaches that advancement to high position does not mean the end of learning. Rather, there is always something to be learned no matter how exalted or powerful someone is. A good motto for a CEO's desk. If she happens to be a woman, change this to **bona femina** (BAW-nah FAY-mih-nah) **semper tiro**.

bos in lingua
bohs ihn LIHN-gwaah
a reason for holding one's tongue

This splendid trope, literally "an ox on the tongue," is used to indicate a weighty reason for silence. "Why are they so quiet?" "Surely they have *bos in lingua*."

bracchium civile
BRAHK-khih-yuum kee-VEE-leh
the civil arm *or* civil power

Of the government, that is. Also given as **bracchium saeculare** (sī-kuu-LAAH-reh), with the same meaning.

brevi manu
BREH-wee MAH-noo
offhand

The literal translation is "with a short hand."

brevis esse laboro, obscurus fio
BREH-wihs EHS-seh lah-BOH-roh awb-SKOO-ruus FEE-yoh
in trying to be concise, I become obscure

Horace, in *Ars Poetica*, instructing writers that it is difficult to achieve brevity without sacrificing clarity. Thus Thoreau's line: "Not that the story need be long, but it will take a long while to make it short."

brevis oratio penetrat caelum
BREH-wihs oh-RAAH-tih-yoh PEH-neh-traht KĪ-luum
a brief prayer reaches heaven

And by extension, brevity in any message is both welcome and effective.

C

caecus amor sui
KĪ-kuus AH-mawr SUU-wee
blind love of self

We have all grown up knowing that love is blind, enabling us to overlook undesirable traits in our beloveds—surely a happy condition. Here, however, Horace tells us that even self-love can be blind—surely not a happy condition. Narcissists, beware.

caelitus mihi vires
KĪ-lih-tuus MIH-hih WEE-rays
my strength is from heaven

Worth believing if you don't stretch it too far.

Caesar non supra grammaticos
KĪ-sahr nohn SUU-praah grahm-MAH-tih-kohs
every last one of us should speak and write correctly

This dictum, "Caesar is not above the grammarians," is taken to show the deep respect that Romans had for their language and literature—even the emperor was expected to handle words with care. Suetonius wrote of an incident in which Tiberius, a first-century Roman emperor, made a grammatical error in a speech. When one of his favorites said it couldn't have been an error because Tiberius was the one who used the locution in dispute, a grammarian replied TU ENIM, CAESAR, CIVITATEM DARE POTES HOMINIBUS, VERBA NON POTES (too EH-nihm KĪ-sahr kee-wih-TAAH-tehm DAH-reh PAW-tehs haw-MIH-nih-buus WEHR-bah nohn PAW-tehs), "You, Caesar, can designate men as citizens, but not make words." Two good thoughts—*Caesar non supra* and TU ENIM, CAESAR—to interject when modern American political leaders massacre the English language.

calceus maior (or major) subvertit
KAHL-keh-yuus MAH-yawr suub-WEHR-tiht
don't get too big for your britches

This metaphorical warning, "a shoe too large trips," may be directed at overly aggressive power-grabbers as well as at entrepreneurs with big eyes. It suggests that enterprises may fall apart because they become too large and unwieldy. Thus, when an already huge conglomerate goes after its umpteenth acquisition, the prudent financial adviser may cite *calceus maior subvertit.*

callida iunctura (or junctura)
KAHL-lih-dah yoonk-TOO-rah
skillful workmanship

This phrase of Horace may also be taken as "skillful joining," with "joining" referring to the work of a cabinetmaker. More broadly, *callida iunctura* may be used as an expression of admiration for any activity accomplished with great skill.

calvo turpius est nihil comato
KAHL-woh TUUR-pih-yuus ehst NIH-hihl kaw-MAAH-toh
don't pretend to be more than you are

One growth industry in our century thrives on developing lotions intended to encourage hair to sprout on men's heads, on transplanting hair when the lotions don't work, and on supplying wigs when other measures fail. Martial's observation to Romans, freely rendered as "there's nothing more unsightly than a bald man with a wig," is directed at those who pretend—whether out of vanity or the desire to deceive—to be more than they really are. The adjective *comatus* translates literally as "longhaired," so *calvo turpius est nihil comato* may also be taken as "there's nothing more unsightly than a long-haired bald man."

candida pax
KAHN-dih-dah paahks
radiant peace

Ovid characterizing peace among nations, the blessed condition following cessation of warfare. The adjective *candida* is translated variously as "white," "bright," "beautiful," "fair," and "clothed in white," as well as "radiant." Take your choice. 'Tis a cessation devoutly to be wished.

candide et constanter
KAHN-dih-day eht kohn-STAHN-tehr
frankly and firmly

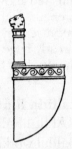

canis in praesepi
KAH-nihs ihn prī-SAY-pee
dog in the manger

This expression is traceable to Aesop's fable in which a dog stations itself near a pile of hay in order to prevent an ox from eating the hay even though the dog itself doesn't eat hay. Thus, *canis in praesepi*, more accurately "dog in the stable," characterizes the disagreeable person who thinks, "If I can't enjoy something, I'll make sure no one else does." Try using the phrase when next you find yourself in a theater sitting near a potato-chip cruncher who hates the movie being shown and doesn't miss an opportunity to ruin the pleasure of the rest of us.

canis timidus vehementius latrat quam mordet
KAH-nihs TIH-mih-duus weh-heh-MEHN-tih-yuus
LAAH-traht kwahm MAWR-deht
a cowardly dog barks more than it bites

There's accurate insight in this Roman proverb. The trouble is that postal workers don't know whether a barking dog is cowardly. And when we apply the proverb to the threats of human bullies, we can only hope that blusterers won't resort to blows. Maybe, but don't count on it.

cantabit vacuus coram latrone viator
kahn-TAAH-biht WAH-kuu-wuus KOH-rahm lah-TROH-
neh wih-YAAH-tawr

a penniless person has nothing to lose

Juvenal telling us "the traveler with an empty purse will sing in the face of a robber." Those of us who live in crime-ridden cities know better than to take Juvenal literally today. The modern mugger hates nothing more than being told his target has no money at all. Thus the common practice of always carrying an amount of folding money on one's person—enough to satisfy a wretch we encounter, but not so large that the inevitable loss will be sorely felt. We surely have advanced in civility in two millennia.

cantilenam eandem canis
kahn-tih-LAY-nahm eh-YAHN-dehm KAH-nihs

you're singing the same old song

Terence's way of saying "there you go again."

capiat qui capere possit
KAH-pih-yaht kwee KAH-peh-reh PAWS-siht

let him take who can take

capistrum maritale
kah-PIHS-truum mah-rih-TAAH-leh

the woes of matrimony

Juvenal, in a disillusioned view of marriage, speaking literally of "the matrimonial halter." If the reader is not certain of the intended sense of "halter," let it be known that *capistrum* can also be translated as "muzzle." Need we go further?

captantes capti sumus
kahp-TAHN-tays KAHP-tee SUU-muus

the tables have been turned

A marvelous idiom, literally "we catchers have been caught," more loosely rendered as "the biters are bitten." All by way of giving the lie to the American adage "never try to con a con man."

captatio benevolentiae
kahp-TAAH-tih-yoh beh-neh-waw-LEHN-tih-yī
laying it on thick

This expression, literally "catching at goodwill," more idiomatically "currying favor," encapsulates the central tactic of the sycophant.

captus nidore culinae
KAHP-tuus nee-DOH-reh kuu-LEE-nī
irresistibly sucked in

Juvenal's colorful way of explaining loss of willpower in the face of great temptation, literally "captivated by the aroma of the kitchen." We can conjure up any number of situations in which the metaphor can be applied, always certain that it will surpass the pedestrian "I just couldn't help myself."

caput lupinum
KAH-puut luu-PEE-nuum
sign of the outlaw

In Old English law, a person who was declared an outlaw—*caput lupinum*, literally "a wolf's head"—could legally be hunted down and killed by anyone who came upon him. The words decreeing outlawry were **caput gerat** (GEHH-raht) **lupinum**, "let him wear the wolf's head," that is, treat him as you would a wild beast.

carent quia vate sacro
KAAH-rehnt KWIH-yah WAAH-teh SAH-kroh
golden words are needed

Horace's phrase, literally "because they lack an inspired bard," explaining that a nation will be forgotten if it is not blessed with the presence of a gifted poet to record the accomplishments of its people.

caret initio et fine
KAAH-reht ih-nih-tih-yoh eht FEE-neh
it lacks beginning and end

Literary critics reviewing a less-than-perfect work need say no more.

carmen triumphale
KAHR-mehn trih-yuum-PHAAH-leh
a song of triumph

carmina morte carent
KAHR-mih-nah MAWR-teh KAAH-rehnt
songs are exempt from death

A line from Ovid asserting that good poetry never dies.

carpent tua poma nepotes
KAHR-pehnt TUU-wah POH-mah neh-POH-tays
plan for the future

In suggesting literally that "your grandsons will gather your apples," Virgil is telling us that hard work and careful management of our resources will pay off long after we are gone. But *nepotes*, "grandchildren," may also be translated as "descendants" or as "spendthrifts." The third translation of *nepotes* is enough to send chills up our spines, making us wonder whether we blunder in planning carefully for future generations, who can be expected to waste the resources passed on to them.

carpere et colligere
KAHR-peh-reh eht kawl-LIH-geh-reh
to pluck and gather

cassis tutissima virtus
KAHS-sihs too-TIHS-sih-mah WIHR-toos
an honest man need fear nothing

This proverb, literally "virtue is the securest helmet," suggests the efficacy of playing the game of life by the rules. What it fails to recognize is that the rules may change, depending on who writes and administers them.

casus fortuitus
KAAH-suus fohr-tuu-WEE-tuus
a matter of chance

In addition to "a matter of chance," *casus fortuitus* is variously translated, for example, as "an inevitable accident" and "a fortuitous occurrence." The final translation is the least satisfactory for the modern reader who may employ the English word "fortuitous" as a synonym for "fortunate." In the best modern usage, a fortuitous occurrence is not intended to denote a fortunate occurrence. Although many writers and speakers may use "fortunate" and "fortuitous" interchangeably, they cannot alter the meaning of the Latin *fortuitus*, whose meaning can best be seen by citing yet another appropriate translation of *casus fortuitus*, "an act of God." This English phrase, often employed in insurance policies, denotes an accident over which people have no control—lightning, hurricane, flood, and the like. Surely, none of these phenomena can be considered fortunate.

casus necessitatis
KAAH-suus neh-kehs-sih-TAAH-tihs
a case of necessity

causa latet, vis est notissima
KOW-sah LAH-teht wees ehst noh-TIHS-sih-mah
the cause is hidden, its force is very well known

An observation of Ovid's applicable to many occurrences and human proclivities. Consider, for example, the rapid growth of juvenile criminal behavior in modern times. Despite the plethora of scholarly and simplistic explanations offered by experts and nonexperts, juvenile criminality is still an instance of *causa latet, vis est notissima.*

cavendo tutus
kah-WEHN-doh TOO-tuus
keep your wits about you

Surely an apt prescription, literally "safe by taking heed," for those who live in potentially dangerous places: "Remember, whenever you go out, *cavendo tutus.*"

cave ne cadas
KAH-way nay KAH-daahs
the bigger they come, the harder they fall

This advice, literally "beware lest thou fall," is most apt for anyone who has achieved a position of some prominence, whether real or imagined. Underlying this locution is the thought that people who rise may later fall, and so it behooves the risers to be nice to the nonrisers they pass on the way, for the risers may meet the nonrisers again on the way down, when the risers themselves have become fallers. And, of course, the higher people rise, the more people they pass on the way up. The jocular "the bigger they come, the harder they fall" is a commonly used English version of *cave ne cadas* but has a different ultimate meaning. "The bigger they come . . ." alludes to how far a knocked-out prizefighter will fall on his way to the canvas. The saying is variously attributed to well-known prizefighters of the past boasting that they fought and beat bigger and heavier opponents. (See also CELSAE GRAVIORE CASU DECIDUNT TURRES.)

cave tibi a cane muto et aqua silenti
KAH-way TIH-bih aah KAH-neh MOO-toh eht
AH-kwaah sih-LEHN-tee
beware of a silent dog and still water

No one knows the underlying nature of either, so the wise person keeps his or her distance.

celeritas et veritas
keh-LEH-rih-taahs eht WAY-rih-taahs
promptness and truth

celsae graviore casu decidunt turres
KEL-sī grah-wih-YOH-reh KAAH-soo DAY-kih-duunt
TUUR-rays
the bigger they come, the harder they fall

Horace advising caution, literally "lofty towers fall with a greater crash," for those on the way up in their careers. This is the same advice given by CAVE NE CADAS, "beware lest you fall," but Horace put the message metaphorically, as befits a poet. Incidentally, *celsae*, "lofty," may also be translated as "haughty" when applied to people.

censor librorum
KAYN-sawr lih-BROH-ruum
a censor of books

An occupational title still to be found in modern times.

censor morum
KAYN-sawr MOH-ruum
a censor

Not someone you especially want to know, literally "the regulator of morals," but someone the Romans had to be wary of.

Another phrase with the same meaning is **custos** (KUUS-tohs, "guardian") **morum**.

certamina divitiarum
kehr-TAAH-mih-nah dee-wih-tih-YAAH-ruum
strivings after wealth

Horace's phrase for the all-consuming struggles—*certamina* also means "battles"—for wealth that dominate the lives of too many people and prevent them from focusing on more laudable and more humane pursuits.

certaminis gaudia
kehr-TAAH-mih-nihs GOW-dih-yah
the joys of battle

Yes, Virginia, there were Romans who relished a good fight.

certum voto pete finem
KEHR-tuum WOH-toh PEH-teh FEE-nehm
don't reach for the moon

Realistic advice from Horace, literally "seek a definite limit to your desire." And then be satisfied with what you achieve. What would Horace have thought of modern financial moguls, movie stars, and baseball players whose annual incomes exceed the gross national products of some nations?

cetera quis nescit?
KAY-teh-rah kwihs NAYS-kiht
who does not know the rest?

Ovid's phrase giving us a way to terminate a recounting of an opponent's misdeeds by suggesting that there is a lot more to tell, but everybody already knows all about it. At least that is what is implied.

cicatrix manet
kih-KAAH-treeks MAH-neht
the memory lingers on

Human psyches being what they are, we may apparently recover from a bad experience, but *cicatrix manet*, literally "the scar remains." And what kinds of bad experiences are these that scar us? Being thrashed by a schoolyard bully, being jilted by a lover, failing to make the varsity football team or cheerleading squad, being laid off by an employer—the list is endless. (See also ETIAM SANATO VULNERE CICATRIX MANET.)

cineri gloria sero venit
KIH-neh-ree GLOH-rih-yah SAY-roh WEH-niht
glory paid to one's ashes comes too late

Martial's epigram telling us not to wait until someone is dead before offering praise.

circuitus verborum
kihr-KUU-wih-tuus wehr-BOH-ruum
a circumlocution

circulus in definiendo
KIHR-kuu-luus ihn day-fee-nih-YEHN-doh
a circular definition

This phrase, literally "a circle in defining," is the particular concern of the lexicographer. A circular definition is a faulty form of definition, in which the definition includes the term being defined—a real no-no. Thus, even though anyone with even a rudimentary knowledge of English knows what the word "door" means, the definer of the word must struggle to accomplish the task ever mindful of the peril of *circulus in definiendo*. Consider, for example, the bravura performance of the scholars who wrote the great *Oxford English Dictionary*. Making certain to avoid *circulus in definiendo,* they defined "door" as "a movable barrier of wood or other material, consisting either of one piece, or of several pieces framed together, usually turning on hinges or sliding in a groove, and serving to close or open a passage into a building, room, etc."

circulus in probando
KIHR-kuu-luus ihn praw-BAHN-doh
circular reasoning

This term, literally "a circle in proving," is also called "reasoning in a circle." It denotes a faulty form of reasoning in which the conclusion itself is assumed as one of the premises. For example, consider "You can't expect poor people ever to rise out of poverty, because poverty cannot be overcome."

citius venit periculum cum contemnitur
KIH-tih-yuus WEH-niht peh-REE-kuu-luum kuum kawn-TEHM-nih-tuur
don't hide your head in the sand

Good advice to all, literally "danger comes sooner when it is not feared," and you ignore this advice at your own peril.

cito maturum, cito putridum
KIH-taw maah-TOO-ruum KIH-taw PUU-trih-duum
quickly ripe, quickly rotten

Fruit, economies, love affairs, novelists, business enterprises—and tennis players—should be permitted to develop slowly.

civis Romanus sum
KEE-wihs roh-MAAH-nuus suum
Ich bin ein Berliner

President John F. Kennedy, alluding to Cicero's proud declaration—literally "I am a Roman citizen." Kennedy's implication paralleled that of Cicero: Citizens (Germans as well as Romans) have political rights, and those rights are not to be denied.

clarum et venerabile nomen
KLAH-ruum eht weh-neh-RAAH-bih-leh NOH-mehn
an illustrious and venerable name

A phrase from Lucan to use when extolling someone truly distinguished. He was recalling Pompey, the great Roman general and statesman. Anyone to whom this phrase is accurately applied is surely in good company.

clavam extorquere Herculi
KLAAH-wahm ehks-TAWR-kweh-reh HEHR-kuu-lee
to move mountains

A colorful way, literally "to wrest away Hercules's club," to describe a well-nigh impossible task that demands great courage as well as extraordinary strength.

cognatio movit invidiam
kawg-NAAH-tih-yoh MAW-wiht ihn-WIH-dih-yahm
kinship promotes ill feeling

An indication that Roman families—not unlike some families today—did not enjoy uninterrupted good feelings. Perhaps members of a family get to know too much about one another.

colloquio iam tempus adest
kawl-LAW-kwih-yoh yahm TEHM-puus AHD-ehst
let's talk

Ovid telling us that "now the time for conversation is at hand."

colluvies vitiorum
kawl-LUU-wih-yays wih-tih-YOH-ruum
an unsavory collection

This phrase, literally "dregs of vice," provides an excellent characterization of any institution one may choose to denigrate—

a state legislature, a municipal government, professional boxing, drug pushers, college athletic scholarship programs, etc.

colubrem in sinu fovere
KAW-luu-brehm ihn SIH-noo faw-WAY-reh
to cherish a serpent in one's bosom

This colorful phrase had its origin in Greek folklore. A farmer one morning picked up a frozen snake and put it into his bosom to warm it up. When the creature was revived by the warmth of the farmer's body, it promptly bit the farmer. Enough to make some of us turn away from a person in need.

columna bellica
kaw-LUUM-nah BEHL-lih-kah
war column *or* war memorial

comes iucundus (or jucundus) in via pro vehiculo est
KAW-mehs yoo-KUUN-duus ihn wih-yaah proh weh-HIH-kuu-loh ehst
an agreeable companion on the road is as good as a carriage

Publilius Syrus telling us that on a long journey pleasant company helps time pass.

comitas gentium
KAW-mih-taahs GEHN-tih-yuum
comity of nations

Also given as **comitas inter gentes** (IHN-tehr GEHN-tays), "between nations." Affability between nations is the basis for diplomacy.

commodum ex iniuria (or **injuria**) sua nemo habere debet

KAWM-maw-duum ehks ihn-YOO-rih-yaah SUU-waah
NAY-moh hah-BAY-reh DAY-beht

no one should profit from his own wrongdoing

A popular opinion in modern times.

commune periculum concordiam parit

kawm-MOO-neh peh-REE-kuu-luum kawn-KAWR-dih-yahm PAH-riht

common danger creates unity

Nothing like a good scare to get people to forget their petty differences and work together for the common good.

communis sensus

kawm-MOO-nihs SAYN-suus

common opinion

The best way for parties to a dispute to end their disagreement. Also taken as "common consent."

compendia dispendia

kawm-PEHN-dih-yah dihs-PEHN-dih-yah

shortcuts are losses

This aphorism encourages care and thoroughness in any undertaking lest an urge to cut corners result in botched work and lead only to starting all over again. In a narrower sense, motorists who go out of their way to save time may in the long run lose time.

compesce mentem

kawm-PAYS-keh MEHN-tehm

control your temper

In literal translation, as "suppress feelings," this advice from Horace may not be sound from the point of view of mental health experts, but when taken to mean "control your temper," it cannot be faulted.

componere lites
kawm-POH-neh-reh LEE-tays
to settle disputes

See also TANTAS COMPONERE LITES.

compos voti
KAWM-pohs WOH-tee
having gotten one's wish

concedo
kawn-KAY-doh
I concede

A term in logic employed to grant that an opponent's argument is superior to one's own. (See also MAIORI CEDO.)

concordia discors
kawn-KAWR-dih-yah DIHS-kawrs
discordant harmony

A marvelous oxymoron coined by Horace that today would be useful in referring to conditions prevalent in many nations. Modern democracies appear always to be practicing—and profiting from—a form of *concordia discors*.

confido et conquiesco
kohn-FEE-doh eht kawn-kwih-YAYS-koh
I trust and am at peace

coniunctis (or conjunctis) viribus

kawn-YOONK-tees WEE-rih-buus

in complete cooperation

This phrase, literally "with united powers," identifies the much-desired condition that a well-organized enterprise strives for in order to succeed.

conquiescat in pace

kawn-kwih-YAYS-kaht ihn PAAH-keh

may he (or she) rest in peace

This final thought is identical in meaning with the more familiar **requiescat** (reh-kwih-YAYS-kaht) **in pace**.

conscia mens recti

KOHN-skih-yah mayns RAYK-tee

someone who knows right from wrong

Ovid's phrase, literally "a mind conscious of rectitude."

conscientia mille testes

kohn-skih-YEHN-tih-yah MEEL-leh TEHS-tays

conscience is worth a thousand witnesses

But not in a court of justice.

consensus tollit errorem

kohn-SAYN-suus TAWL-liht ehr-ROH-rehm

agreement removes uncertainty

Decisions are easy when all parties to a debate agree.

consequitur quodcumque petit

kohn-SEH-kwih-tuur kwawd-KUUM-kweh PEH-tiht

he attains whatever he attempts

Literally, "it gets whatever it seeks." Ovid used this expression to describe a magic hunting spear that always struck its prey. The phrase may also be applied to a ruthless person who will stop at nothing to gain success.

consilio et animis
kohn-SIH-lih-yoh eht AH-nih-mees
by wisdom and courage

Another self-adulatory motto to emblazon on your family coat of arms—if you find it appropriate. (For additional mottoes, see the next three entries as well as AUDACTER ET SINCERE and AUDAX ET CAUTUS.)

consilio et prudentia
kohn-SIH-lih-yoh eht proo-DEHN-tih-yah
by wisdom and prudence

consilio, non impetu
kohn-SIH-lih-yoh nohn IHM-peh-too
by deliberation *or* wisdom, not by impulse

constantia et virtute
kohn-STAHN-tih-yah eht wihr-TOO-teh
by firmness and courage

consuetudo est optima interpres legum
kohn-sway-TOO-doh ehst AWP-tih-mah ihn-TEHR-prehs LAY-guum
custom is the best interpreter of laws

When existing statutes are vague, or when no statutes apply to a matter at hand, justice is best served by considering the customs of a community. (See also CONSUETUDO PRO LEGE SERVATUR.)

consuetudo loci observanda est
kohn-sway-TOO-doh LAW-kee awb-sehr-WAHN-dah ehst
when in Rome, do as the Romans do

Good advice, literally "the custom of the place is to be observed," for any ancient or modern stranger in a strange land.

consuetudo pro lege servatur
kohn-sway-TOO-doh proh LAY-geh sehr-WAAH-tuur
custom is observed as law

This legal maxim reminds us that laws generally have their origin in local customs. (See also CONSUETUDO EST OPTIMA INTERPRES LEGUM.)

consuetudo quasi altera natura
kohn-sway-TOO-doh KWAH-sih AHL-teh-rah naah-TOO-rah
habit is, as it were, second nature

Caesar on the efficacy of routine.

contra felicem vix deus vires habet
KAWN-traah fay-LEE-kehm wihks DEH-yuus WEE-rays HAH-beht
don't bet against a crapshooter on a roll

Publilius Syrus telling us that "against a lucky man a god scarcely has power." Why buck the odds?

contra ius (or jus) gentium
KAWN-traah yoos GEHN-tih-yuum
against the law of nations

contra malum mortis non est medicamen in hortis

KAWN-traah MAH-luum MAWR-tihs nohn ehst meh-dih-KAAH-mehn ihn HAWR-tees

no one wins out against death

A sure bet, literally "against the evil of death there is no remedy in the gardens." And if we are to take literally the last word of this observation—*hortis*, "in the gardens"—not even herbal remedies will do any good.

contra mundum

KAWN-traah MUUN-duum

against the world

Brave souls—at best dreamers, at worst fools—who stand *contra mundum* are those who defy prevailing opinion.

contra negantem principia non est disputandum

KAWN-traah neh-GAHN-tehm preen-KIH-pih-yah nohn ehst dihs-puu-TAHN-duum

there's no arguing with one who denies first principles

The validity of this observation cannot be denied. Consider the incoherent rantings of people who ignore well-established facts and human experience to argue for their political or social agendas.

copia verborum

KOH-pih-yah wehr-BOH-ruum

prolixity

The condition of wordiness, literally "abundance of words," also given as **copia fandi** (FAHN-dee), "abundance of talk." Whichever phrase is used, this boring phenomenon must be stamped out. Readers and listeners of the world, unite!

cor ad cor loquitur
kawr ahd kawr LAW-kwih-tuur
heart speaks to heart

Surely there is no better way to speak than heart to heart. *Cor ad cor loquitur* was the motto of John Henry Newman, known usually as Cardinal Newman. He was a nineteenth-century Anglican theologian who converted to Catholicism in 1845 and in 1879 was made a cardinal. (See his epitaph, EX UM-BRIS ET IMAGINIBUS IN VERITATEM.)

coram paribus
KOH-rahm PAH-rih-buus
before equals

In the democratic tradition, we expect that a jury trial will be held *coram paribus,* best translated as "before one's peers." Peers in this sense are persons having the same legal status as the person on trial. They are not required to be the equals of the person on trial in any other sense.

cor illi in genua decidit
kawr IHL-lee ihn GEH-nuu-wah DAY-kih-diht
he (or she) is scared stiff

Literally "his heart falls into his knees," and we all know that knees are said to shake when someone is extremely frightened.

cor ne edito
kawr nay AY-dih-toh
share your troubles with a pal or therapist

Excellent advice, literally "eat not thy heart," in a Latin translation of a phrase attributed to Pythagoras, the sixth-century B.C. Greek philosopher. Rather than eat your heart out in silence, he said, open up to someone you trust. You'll feel better.

corpora lente augescunt cite exstinguuntur

KAWR-paw-rah LEHN-tay ow-GAYS-kuunt KIH-tay ehks-stihn-GWUUN-tuur

we grow slowly, die quickly

Tacitus making a depressing observation, literally "bodies are slow in growth, rapid in decay."

corpus valet sed aegrotat crumena

KAWR-puus WAH-leht sehd ī-GROH-taht kruu-MAY-nah

what good is health if you can't afford to enjoy it?

We are accustomed to hearing that health is better than wealth, but now we hear the complaint in *corpus valet sed aegrotat crumena* that "the body is well, but the purse is sick." The inference is clear: health without the money to enjoy it is not all it's cracked up to be.

corruptio optimi pessima

kawr-RUUP-tih-yoh AWP-tih-mee PEHS-sih-mah

corruption of the best is worst

When bank tellers are caught with their hands in the cookie jar, provided their pilferings are small, we can perhaps forgive them for succumbing to petty temptations. But when, for example, a scientist, like Shakespeare's soldier "seeking the bubble reputation," is caught fudging experimental data—that is a different matter. It is in this spirit that we may understand *corruptio optimi pessima*.

corruptissima in republica plurimae leges

kawr-ruup-TIHS-sih-maah ihn ray-POO-blih-kaah PLOO-rih-mī LAY-gays

the more corrupt the state, the more numerous the laws

Tacitus hit this one on the nose. Every time a government tries to strengthen its laws, the enemies of the state find new ways to cheat—with the assistance of clever lawyers, accountants, and lobbyists—which inevitably lead to more and more laws, and less and less observance of the laws. And so on.

crambe repetita
KRAHM-bay reh-peh-TEE-tah
warmed-over cabbage

Juvenal's evocative phrase for any story we have been subjected to time after time after time, and for any literary work made stale by repetition. While *crambe repetita* is well translated as "stale repetitions," the word *crambe* alone is literally translated as "cabbage," and everyone who knows cabbage realizes that it stinks after it has been cooked too long.

cras credemus, hodie nihil
kraahs kray-DAY-muus HAW-dih-yay NIH-hihl
tomorrow we'll believe, today not

Often interpreted as "small minds are closed to new ideas."

cras mihi
kraahs MIH-hih
my turn tomorrow

The motto of any younger sibling. After all, fair is fair. A related phrase, but not as generous, is **hodie mihi, cras tibi** (HAW-dih-yay MIH-hih kraahs TIH-bih), "my turn today, yours tomorrow."

crassa neglegentia
KRAHS-sah nehg-leh-GEHN-tih-yah
gross negligence

A legal term implying culpability for the perpetrator of the act so characterized.

crede experto
KRAY-deh ehks-PEHR-toh
believe the experienced person

Also given as EXPERTO CREDE, with the same meaning. It must be understood that we are not being advised to believe an expert. Today's experts too often turn out to be little more than persons paid to agree with the person who hires them. The adjective **expertus** (ehks-PEHR-tuus) and its inflected forms mean "experienced."

crede quod habes, et habes
KRAY-deh kwawd HAH-bays eht HAH-bays
think positively

A plug for self-confidence, literally "believe that you have it, and you have it."

crede ut intellegas
KRAY-deh uut ihn-TEHL-leh-gaahs
believe so that you may understand

This injunction is directed at those who seek a basis for their faith or the faith they seek, implying that faith does not begin with understanding, but ends in understanding.

credite posteri
KRAY-dih-teh PAWS-teh-ree
you'd better believe it!

Horace exhorting future generations to believe what he has written. His message translates literally as "believe it, later generations!" A memoirist would do well to write *credite posteri* at the head of an opening chapter.

credula res amor est
KRAY-duu-lah rays AH-mawr ehst
people in love will believe anything

Ovid, a keen observer, telling us "a credulous thing is love." So what else is new?

crescit amor nummi quantum ipsa pecunia crescit
KRAYS-kiht AH-mawr NUUM-mee KWAHN-tuum IHP-sah peh-KOO-nih-yah KRAYS-kiht
the more you have, the more you want

Juvenal's dismal observation, literally "the love of money grows as wealth increases," makes it clear that avarice has been with us at least since the time of ancient Rome, and there's no containing it. How else to explain the modern phenomenon of rapidly growing wealth of the already wealthy while more and more people sink deeper into poverty?

crescit sub pondere virtus
KRAYS-kiht suub PAWN-deh-reh WIHR-toos
virtue grows under oppression

Adversity often brings out the best in people.

cribro aquam haurire
KREE-broh AH-kwahm how-REE-reh
to draw water in a sieve

A hopeless pursuit. Don't waste your time in unproductive effort.

crimen falsi
KREE-mehn FAHL-see
the crime of forgery

This phrase may also be translated as "the crime of false-hood."

crimen laesae maiestatis (or majestatis)
KREE-mehn LĪ-sī maah-yehs-TAAH-tihs

high treason

A legal term denoting what was formerly called the crime of lese majesty, an offense against the dignity of a ruler. Back when kings were kings, this was a matter of utmost seriousness. Today, with kings usually out of the picture, any high treason is directed against the state.

crux
kruuks

cross

The word *crux* has several meanings in addition to "cross." For example, it can be translated as "gallows," "perplexing problem," "puzzle," or "torment" and appears in several phrases: **crux criticorum** (krih-tih-KOH-ruum), "of critics"; **crux interpretum** (ihn-TEHR-preh-tuum), "of translators or interpreters"; **crux mathematicorum** (mah-thay-mah-tih-KOH-ruum), "of mathematicians"; and **crux medicorum** (meh-dih-KOH-ruum), "of physicians." Any of the five meanings supplied here for *crux* may be used in interpreting these phrases.

cucullus non facit monachum
kuu-KUUL-luus nohn FAH-kiht MAW-nah-khuum

the cowl does not make the monk

This proverb tells us not to be deceived by mere trappings. It takes more than a toque to make a good chef, for example, and more than a tutu to make a fine ballerina. (For a contrary opinion, see VESTIS VIRUM FACIT.)

cui peccare licet, peccat minus
koowee pehk-KAAH-reh LIH-keht PEHK-kaht MIH-nuus

one who is free to sin, sins less

Wise words from Ovid.

cuique suum
KOOWEE-kweh SUU-wuum
to each his own

cuius est divisio, alterius est electio
KUU-yuus ehst dee-WEE-sih-yoh ahl-teh-REE-yuus ehst
ay-LAYK-tih-yoh
one cuts the pie, the other has the first slice

Very practical advice is given here, literally "whichever (of two parties) makes the division, the other makes the choice." When a partnership—a marriage, for example—must be dissolved, disagreement is almost certain to arise over how to split assets held in common. So one party divides the assets, and the other chooses the half he or she desires. Wisdom rivaling Solomon's.

culpae poena par esto
KUUL-pī POY-nah paahr EHS-toh
let the punishment be proportioned to the crime

This principle has long been considered a cornerstone of criminal justice. One problem with it lies in the changing mood of the public, so what once appeared to be appropriate punishment for a given crime may now appear too lenient or too harsh. Nevertheless, recall W.S. Gilbert's lines from *The Mikado*:

> My object all sublime
> I shall achieve in time—
> To make the punishment fit the crime.

(See also NOXIAE POENA PAR ESTO.)

culpa lata
KUUL-pah LAAH-tah
gross neglect

A term in law, as opposed to **culpa levis** (LEH-wihs), "excusable neglect."

culpam maiorum (or majorum) posteri luunt
KUUL-pahm mah-YOH-ruum PAWS-teh-ree LUU-wuunt
the sins of the fathers

A sobering observation, literally "descendants pay for the shortcomings of their ancestors." What we say and do may affect future generations. (See also VIVIMUS IN POSTERIS.)

culpam poena premit comes
KUUL-pahm POY-nah PREH-miht KAW-mehs
punishment presses hard upon crime as its companion

Horace warning anyone contemplating commission of a crime that crime does not pay. Modern criminals apparently don't read Horace.

cum bona venia
kuum BAW-naah WEH-nih-yaah
with your kind indulgence

cum multis aliis
kuum MUUL-tees AH-lih-yees
with many others

cum permissu superiorum
kuum pehr-MEES-soo suu-peh-rih-YOH-ruum
with the permission of superiors

cuneus cuneum trudit
KUU-neh-yuus KUU-neh-yuum TROO-diht
steady effort pays off

The literal meaning of *cuneus cuneum trudit* is "wedge drives wedge." And just as a small opening made by a thin wedge can by persistent effort with additional wedges bring down the largest tree, small beginnings of any kind can eventually lead to great achievement—or to disaster.

currus bovem trahit
KUUR-ruus BAW-wehm TRAH-hiht
don't put the cart before the horse

It's a mistake to deal with minor matters before getting down to the central issue confronting you, as we are warned in *currus bovem trahit*, literally "the wagon drags the ox." In planning any activity, we must keep first things first.

curta supellex
KUUR-tah suu-PEHL-lehks
a meager store of knowledge

The literal meaning of this phrase, "a scanty supply of furniture," provides an interesting characterization of someone who knows little. Now we have a substitute for the tired phrase "no rocket scientist."

D

da dextrum misero
daah DEHKS-truum MIH-seh-roh
extend a hand to the needy

In a time when men and women live on the streets of the self-styled richest nation on earth, this injunction of Virgil, literally "give a right hand to the wretched," is surely appropriate. (See also DATE OBOLUM BELISARIO.)

da locum melioribus
daah LAW-kuum meh-lih-YOH-rih-buus
give way to your betters

Terence asking for respect for superiors.

dante Deo
DAHN-teh DEH-yoh
by the gift of God

dapes inemptae
DAH-pays ihn-aymp-tī
homegrown food

A friendly phrase, literally "feasts unbought," useful for health devotees, fans of organically grown foodstuffs, and protectors of the natural environment—the most assiduous of whom grow their own food for the table.

dare fatis vela
DAH-reh FAAH-tees WAY-lah
to sail where fate directs

Virgil's advice to sailors—and others making their way through life—literally "to give the sails to the fates." Things will probably turn out right. (See also DATA FATA SECUTUS.)

dare pondus idonea fumo
DAH-reh PAWN-duus ih-DOH-neh-yah FOO-moh
absolutely worthless

Persius offering book critics a damning phrase sure not to be quoted in advertisements, literally "fit only to give weight to smoke." Unfortunately, *dare pondus idonea fumo* may evoke images of book burning. Perhaps it is better to say "useful only as a doorstop."

data fata secutus
DAH-tah FAAH-tah seh-KOO-tuus
following what fate decrees

Virgil, Roman to the core, recognizing the power of ineluctable destiny. (See also DARE FATIS VELA.)

date obolum Belisario
DAAH-teh AW-baw-luum beh-lih-SAH-rih-yoh
give alms to a beggar

Belisarius, a great general serving Roman emperor Justinian (sixth century A.D.), was accused of conspiracy to overthrow Justinian and was imprisoned for a few months. It is said unreliably that his captors put his eyes out and Belisarius was reduced to begging. Belisarius is remembered in *date obolum Belisario*, literally "give a penny to Belisarius." An obolus is a Greek coin of little value. (See also DA DEXTRUM MISERO.)

Davus sum, non Oedipus
DAH-wuus suum nohn OY-dih-poos
I'm just an average Joe, not an eye surgeon

This line from Terence, literally "I am Davus, not Oedipus," can be freely translated as "I am an ordinary man, and no solver of riddles like Oedipus." Davus may be thought of as Everyman, while Oedipus, it will be recalled, solved the riddle of the Sphinx:

> What goes on four feet, on two feet, and three,
> But the more feet it goes on the weaker it be?

Oedipus solved the riddle, answering that it was a man: as an infant, he crawls on all fours, in manhood walks erect on two feet, and in old age requires a cane to support his legs.

dea certe
DEH-yah KEHR-tay
assuredly a goddess

A fine compliment to pay any woman of outstanding achievement in her lifetime.

de alieno corio liberalis
day ah-lih-YAY-noh KAW-rih-yoh lee-beh-RAAH-lihs
free with other people's money

Literally "generous with another person's leather."

de auditu
day ow-DEE-too
by hearing *or* hearsay

debellare superbos
day-behl-LAAH-reh suu-PEHR-bohs
to subdue the arrogant

debemur morti nos nostraque
day-BAY-muur MAWR-tee nohs NAWS-trah-kweh
we are destined for death, we and our works

Horace had almost all of this right, but his own works destined for death? Not a chance. (See also DEFICIT OMNE QUOD NASCITUR.)

debitum naturae
DAY-bih-tuum naah-TOO-rī
the debt to nature

A euphemism for death and evocative of "ashes to ashes and dust to dust" in suggesting that all of us are merely on loan to the world.

de bonis propriis
day BAW-nees PRAW-prih-yees
out of one's own pocket

Literally "from one's own goods."

decessit sine prole
day-KEHS-siht SIH-neh PROH-leh
he (or she) died without issue

Childless, that is.

decet imperatorem stantem mori
DEH-keht ihm-peh-rah-TOH-rehm STAHN-tehm MAW-ree
it is fitting that an emperor die standing

Said to be the dying words of the Roman emperor Vespasian (first century A.D.), who is reported to have stood upright while awaiting his death. It is also reported that the upright English queen Elizabeth I (1533–1603) died upright.

decies repetita placebit
DEH-kih-yays reh-peh-TEE-tah plah-KAY-biht
some things are worth hearing over and over again

Literally "though ten times repeated, it will continue to please." Horace tells us that works of quality—poems, plays, or musical compositions—will never pall. He was not alluding to the stale stories told again and again by husbands and other bores.

decipit frons prima multos
DAY-kih-piht frawns PREE-mah MUUL-tohs
beware of first impressions

Wise words from Horace, "the first appearance deceives many," cautioning young people and old fools against precipitate judgments of people they meet—in particular warning against falling in love too fast.

decumanus fluctus
deh-kuu-MAAH-nuus FLUUK-tuus
the Big One

Literally "the tenth wave." An ominous phrase reflecting the ancient and persistent notion that the tenth wave in a recurring natural movement—for example, tidal action or seismic activity—is thought to be by far the largest or most powerful. And Californians pay heed to the Richter scale and count shocks and aftershocks, waiting for the ninth, tenth, eleventh. . . .

de dolo malo
day DAW-loh MAH-loh
from evil intent

A legal term, also translated as "from willful fraud."

deficit omne quod nascitur
DAY-fih-kiht AWM-neh kwawd NAAHS-kih-tuur
nothing is certain but death and taxes

Quintilian calling attention, in case anyone forgets, to the transitory nature of life, literally "everything that is born passes away." It is Benjamin Franklin who is credited with first calling attention to the inevitability of death and taxes. (See also DEBEMUR MORTI NOS NOSTRAQUE.)

de fumo in flammam
day FOO-moh ihn FLAHM-mahm
out of the frying pan into the fire

Surely the English phrase given above, which dates from the sixteenth century, is more striking than its Latin progenitor, literally "out of the smoke into the flame." Whichever you prefer, take care that in trying to get out of a sticky situation you do not immediately fall into a worse one.

degeneres animos timor arguit
day-GEH-neh-rays AH-nih-mohs TIH-mawr AHR-guu-wiht
fear betrays base souls

> Virgil's judgment of cowards

de gratia
day GRAAH-tih-yaah
from favor *or* by favor

When we do anything *de gratia*, we do it "willingly," out of the goodness of our hearts.

deiecta (or dejecta) arbore quivis ligna colligit
day-YEHK-taah AHR-baw-reh KWEE-wees LEEG-nah KAWL-lih-giht
standing by while others struggle

This proverb, literally "when the tree is felled, anyone gathers the wood," tells us that lazy people too often profit from the hard work of others.

Dei sub numine viget
DEH-yee suub NOO-mih-neh WIH-geht
it flourishes under the will of God

> Motto of Princeton University.

de lana caprina
day LAAH-naah kah-PREE-naah
about anything worthless

A phrase adapted from Horace, literally "about goat's wool," used to characterize a worthless discussion or other unproductive activity. Goat's wool is suggestive of worthlessness because goats have hair, not wool. So we may say, "They foolishly spend their time talking *de lana caprina.*" It is interesting to note that *caprina* may also be translated as "underarm odor." (See also RIXATUR DE LANA SAEPE CAPRINA.)

deliberando saepe perit occasio
day-lee-beh-RAHN-doh SĪ-peh PEH-riht awk-KAAH-sih-yoh

let's get down to business

One of the worst things we can do when we are considering a problem that's crying out for a solution is discuss and discuss interminably. Publilius Syrus, here giving us yet another of his compelling observations, tells us literally that "opportunity is often lost by considering too long."

delphinum natare doces
dehl-PHEE-nuum nah-TAAH-reh DAW-kays

you're teaching a dolphin how to swim

This rebuke means "you are teaching an experienced person how to do something he or she already knows how to do." Primarily among the British, this thought is conveyed idiomatically in "you're teaching your grandmother [how] to suck eggs." (See also AQUILAM VOLARE DOCES.)

denique caelum
DAY-nih-kweh KĪ-luum

heaven at last!

Battle cry of the Crusaders of the late Middle Ages.

deorum cibus est
deh-YOH-ruum KIH-buus ehst

it is food for the gods

destitutis ventis remos adhibe

day-stih-TOO-tees WEHN-tees RAY-mohs AHD-hih-bay

try anything, it may work

When disaster threatens, Americans are apt to say, "Don't just sit there. Do something." The Romans had the same thought, expressed literally here as "when the winds fail, take to the oars."

desunt inopiae multa, avaritiae omnia

DAY-suunt ihn-AW-pih-yī MUUL-tah ah-waah-RIH-tih-yī AWM-nih-yah

poverty wants many things, avarice wants everything

Publilius Syrus saying it all about greed.

desunt multa

DAY-suunt MUUL-tah

many things are wanting

detur digniore

DEH-tuur dihg-nih-YOH-reh

let it be given to one more worthy

The Latin appropriate for the rare situation in which one turns down a proffered award.

Deus avertat!

DEH-yuus aah-WEHR-taht

God forbid!

dextras dare

DEHKS-traahs DAH-reh

shake on it

Literally "to give right hands"; more freely, "to shake hands as a pledge of mutual trust."

dextro tempore
DEHKS-troh TEHM-paw-reh
at a favorable *or* lucky moment

The Romans scarcely made a move without consulting a seer, who would tell them whether the time was right for a contemplated action—usually in ambiguous language protective of the seer's reputation for giving reliable advice.

dicamus bona verba
dee-KAAH-muus BAW-nah WEHR-bah
let us speak words of good omen

Literally "let us speak good words."

dicta docta pro datis
DIHK-tah DAWK-tah proh DAH-tees
words are cheap

A thought from Plautus, "clever speeches in place of giving gifts."

dictum ac factum
DIHK-tuum ahk FAHK-tuum
no sooner said than done

Literally "said and done."

dictum de dicto
DIHK-tuum day DIHK-toh
a hearsay report

Literally "a saying from a saying."

dictum sapienti sat est
DIHK-tuum sah-pih-YEHN-tee saht ehst
a word to the wise is sufficient

A proverb attributed to Plautus.

difficilia quae pulchra

dihf-fih-KIH-lih-yah kwī
PUUL-khrah

beautiful things are difficult

> To achieve, that is.

digito monstrari

DIH-gih-toh mohn-STRAAH-
ree

to be a celebrity

> Plautus indicating, literally "to
> be pointed out with the finger,"
> the recognition accorded a famous
> person.

dimidium facti qui coepit habet

dee-MIH-dih-yuum FAHK-tee
kwee KOY-piht HAH-beht

once begun is half done

> Horace urging us to get started,
> literally "he who makes a start has
> half the work done."

di minores

dee mih-NOH-rays

men of second rank

> Literally "lesser gods."

diminuere Priscianis caput

dee-mih-NUU-weh-reh prees-kih-YAAH-nihs KAH-puut

to violate rules of grammar

Priscian was a sixth-century A.D. grammarian at Constanti-
nople whose textbook of Latin grammar was used widely. He is
remembered today for *diminuere Priscianis caput,* literally "to
make Priscian's head smaller," and in its usual English rendering, "to break Priscian's head." Both mean "to be guilty of sole-
cisms."

di pia facta vident
dee PIH-yah FAHK-tah WIH-dehnt
someone is watching

Ovid telling us literally in "the gods see upright deeds" that
whatever good we do will not go unrecognized.

divitiae virum faciunt
dee-WIH-tih-yī WIH-ruum FAH-kih-yuunt
riches make the man

A cynical, but in many circles realistic, view of the world.

domat omnia virtus
DAW-maht AWM-nih-yah WIHR-toos
virtue conquers all things

The Romans made much of virtue, as you surely realize by
now. If, by chance, you have not seen *virtus* until now, turn to
the several entries that begin with this word. (By way of contrast, see also DIVITIAE VIRUM FACIUNT.)

domus et placens uxor
DAW-muus eht PLAH-kayns UUKS-awr
home and a satisfying wife

Horace speaking of all a man needs to be happy. But what
does a woman need? Horace is silent.

domus sua cuique est tutissimum refugium
DAW-muus SUU-wah KOOWEE-kweh ehst too-TIHS-
sih-muum reh-FUU-gih-yuum
everyone's home is his (or her) safest refuge

In an English version of this proverb going back about four
centuries, "a man's home is his castle."

duabus sellis sedere
duu-AAH-buus SEHL-lees seh-DAY-reh
to take both sides in a dispute

This metaphor may be translated more literally as "to be
seated in two seats" or much less than literally as "to wear two
hats."

duas tantum res anxius optat, panem et circenses
DUU-aahs TAHN-tuum rays AAHNKS-ih-yuus AWP-taht
PAAH-nehm eht kihr-KAYN-says
keep the masses fed and entertained

According to Juvenal, the cynical formula for ruling the Roman populace successfully, which may be translated as "two
things only do the people earnestly desire, bread and circus
games."

ducunt volentem fata, nolentem trahunt
DOO-kuunt waw-LEHN-tehm FAAH-tah noh-LEHN-
tehm TRAH-huunt
the fates lead the willing, drag the unwilling

Seneca the Younger on the inevitability of destiny—no matter whether we resist or not, the outcome is the same.

dulce bellum inexpertis
DUUL-keh BEHL-luum ihn-ehks-PEHR-tees
only people who have never served advocate war

A realistic—but surely incorrect—observation, translated nearly literally as "sweet is war to those who have never tried it."

dulce quod utile
DUUL-keh kwawd OO-tih-leh
pleasant is that which is useful

dulcis amor patriae
DUUL-kihs AH-mawr PAH-trih-yī
sweet is the love of one's native land

dum loquor, hora fugit
duum LAW-kwawr HOH-rah FUU-giht
no more talking if I'm to get anything done

Ovid, who knew he had better things to do with his time, saying "time is flying while I speak." (See also AMICI FURES TEMPORIS.)

dummodo sit dives, barbarus ipse placet
DUUM-maw-daw siht DEE-wehs BAHR-bah-ruus IHP-seh PLAH-keht
when money talks, everybody listens

Ovid telling us that people are always willing to put up with anybody who is wealthy, literally "so long as he is rich, even a barbarian is pleasing."

dum vitant stulti vitia in contraria current
duum WEE-tahnt STUUL-tee WIH-tih-yah ihn kawn-TRAAH-rih-yah KUUR-rehnt
in shunning vices, fools run to opposite extremes

Horace telling us to use moderation when attempting to improve our own behavior. One step at a time is better than cold turkey.

duos qui sequitur lepores neutrum capit
DUU-wohs kwee SEH-kwih-tuur LEH-paw-rays
NEHYOO-truum KAH-piht

one who chases two hares catches neither one

One bullet cannot hit two targets.

E

e consensu gentium
ay kohn-SAYN-soo GEHN-tih-yuum

out of general agreement of people

An argument based on general agreement of reasonable people is an **argumentum** (ahr-goo-MEHN-tuum) **e consensu gentium**.

edax rerum
EH-daahks RAY-ruum

gluttonous

Literally "devouring of things," describing the proclivity of voracious eaters. (See also EDO ERGO SUM.) Ovid applied *edax rerum* to time in **tempus** (TEHM-puus) **edax rerum**, usually translated as "time, the devourer of all things."

edo ergo sum
EH-doh EHR-goh suum

I eat, therefore I exist

A sure sign of vitality, since the dead don't eat. *Edo ergo sum* is evocative of the famous axiom of Descartes, **cogito ergo sum** (KOH-gih-toh EHR-goh suum), "I think, therefore I exist."

e flamma petere cibum
ay FLAHM-maah PEH-teh-reh KIH-buum
to live by desperate means

A phrase of Terence, literally "to seek food out of the flame," suggesting the mind-set of people on their uppers who are willing to face any danger in order to survive.

ego spem pretio non emo
EH-goh spehm PREH-tih-yoh nohn EH-moh
show me

Where we might say, "I don't buy a pig in a poke," Terence said, "I don't purchase hope for a price."

eiusdem generis
eh-YUUS-dehm GEH-neh-rihs
of the same kind

The same meaning is conveyed by **eiusdem farinae** (fah-REE-nī), literally "of the same flour." One might describe two criminals, for example, as *eiusdem generis* or *eiusdem farinae*.

eius nulla culpa est cui parere necesse sit
EH-yuus NOOL-lah KUUL-pah ehst koowee pah-RAY-reh neh-KEHS-seh siht
one forced to obey is not at fault

This axiom suggests we go slow in judging anyone who acts under duress. Consider what you and I might do under similar circumstances.

elapso tempore
ay-LAAHP-soh TEHM-paw-reh
the time having elapsed

elephantum ex musca facis
eh-leh-PHAHN-tuum ehks MUUS-kaah FAH-kihs
you're making a mountain out of a molehill

> Literally "you're making an elephant out of a fly."

elephantus non capit murem
eh-leh-PHAHN-tuus nohn KAH-piht MOO-rehm
an elephant does not capture a mouse

> This saying, translated literally above, can be taken to mean "important people don't occupy themselves with trifles." It can also mean "be sure to use an appropriate tool (or punishment) to achieve the purpose you have in mind."

empta dolore docet experientia
AYMP-tah daw-LOH-reh DAW-keht ehks-peh-rih-YEHN-tih-yah
experience bought with pain teaches effectively.

> At least that's the theory. Do we really learn from our mistakes? (See also EVENTUS STULTORUM MAGISTER.)

e multis paleis paulum fructus collegi
ay MUUL-tees PAH-leh-yees POW-lahm FROOK-toos kawl-LAY-gee
a few pearls of wisdom scattered in a desert of words

> This observation, literally "from much chaff I have gathered a little grain," expresses the disappointment we often feel after wading through a tedious book or article and finding only a few worthwhile thoughts.

emunctae naris
ay-MUUNK-tī NAAH-rihs
of mature judgment

Horace, in characterizing a person of keen judgment or perception, hit it right on the nose with *emunctae naris*, literally "of cleared nostril" or "with blown nose." This phrase may be applied to anyone having the expertise to judge—not only sniff—the quality of something presented for appraisal.

Epicuri de grege porcus
eh-pih-KOO-ree day GREH-geh PAWR-kuus
a glutton

Horace's phrase, "a hog from the drove of Epicurus." Epicurus (341–270 B.C.), a Greek philosopher and moral theorist, was given a bum rap when his moral theory—seeking the minimization of pain by avoidance of unnecessary fears and desires—which we call Epicureanism, began to be perceived in the popular mind as advocating riotous living and indulgence of the appetites. Thus the meaning "a glutton" given above.

epistola non erubescit
eh-PIHS-taw-lah nohn ay-ruu-BAYS-kiht
easier to put it in writing

We can put things in letters and even in text messages and e-mails—for example, expressions of admiration, love, rejection, or hatred—that we may find difficult to say directly to someone. Thus Cicero's advice, literally "a letter does not blush," on the advantages of writing letters.

equi frenato est auris in ore
EH-kwee fray-NAAH-toh ehst OW-rihs ihn OH-reh
what to do when someone won't listen

When words are not heeded, a show of force may be needed to get someone's attention. As Horace put it in this adage, literally "the ear of a horse is in its bridled mouth," the only recourse may be to inflict some pain. Thus, it is not always worthwhile to constantly forgive and forget.

e re nata
ay ray NAAH-taah
as matters stand

A useful phrase from Apuleius, also interpreted as "under the circumstances," "as things are," "on the spur of the moment," and "at once."

ergo bibamus!
EHR-goh bih-BAAH-muus
let's break out a bottle!

A call for merrymaking, literally "therefore, let us drink," that may go out when a big project—for example, the tedious copying of a text by a monk or the writing of a Ph.D. dissertation—is finally completed. Also expressed as **nunc est bibendum** (nuunk ehst bih-BEHN-duum), "now it is time to drink."

eripuit caelo fulmen sceptrumque tyrannis
ay-RIH-puu-wiht KĪ-loh FUUL-mehn skayp-TRUUM-kweh tü-RAHN-nees
he snatched the thunderbolt from heaven and the scepter from tyrants

The legend was adapted from Manilius, the first-century author of a scientific work called the *Astronomica*. It was inscribed under a bust of Benjamin Franklin—our famous diplomat and kite flier—that was sculpted by Jean-Antoine Houdon in 1778. Manilius explains that scientific knowledge can free human beings from irrational fears, such as the belief that a thunderbolt portended the anger of the gods. Franklin was equally famous for advancing our knowledge of electricity by snatching a thunderbolt from the sky as well as for snatching away power from tyrannical rulers.

est ars etiam male dicendi
ehst ahrs EH-tih-yahm MAH-lay dee-KEHN-dee
there's an art even to speaking evil

Advice to the heavy-handed derogator.

est deus in nobis
ehst DEH-yuus ihn NOH-bees
there is a god within us

Ovid reminding us that good and the capability to do worth-while things reside in all of us.

esto quod esse videris
EHS-toh kwawd EHS-seh wih-DAY-rihs
be what you seem to be

Avoiding pretense makes life easier all around.

est quaedam flere voluptas
ehst KWĪ-dahm FLAY-reh waw-LUUP-taahs
there is a certain pleasure in weeping

Insight from Ovid.

estque pati poenas quam meruisse minus
EHST-kweh PAAH-tee POY-naahs kwahm meh-ruu-WIHS-seh MIH-nuus
it's better to suffer punishment than to deserve it

Ovid telling us to face the music instead of living in dread.

esurienti ne occurras
ay-suur-ih-YEHN-tee nay awk-KUUR-raahs
don't take on an impoverished opponent

This maxim, literally "don't attack a hungry person," cautions us that even the weak may become dangerous when impelled by severe privation.

et alibi
eht AH-lih-bee
and elsewhere

This phrase—like **et alii** (AH-lih-yee), "and other men"; **et aliae** (AH-lih-yī), "and other women"; and **et alia** (AH-lih-yah), "and other things"—is abbreviated **et al**.

et ego in Arcadia
eht EH-goh ihn ahr-KAH-dih-yaah
I have known true contentment

Arcadia, a region of southern Greece, epitomized rural happiness, so this statement, literally "I too have been in Arcadia," can be read to indicate contentment with one's past life. Yet, when used as a tombstone inscription, it can be read as "I (Death) am even in Arcadia," indicating that death is everywhere. As though we didn't already know it.

et genus et formam regina pecunia donat
eht GEH-nuus eht FAWR-mahm ray-GEE-nah peh-KOO-nih-yah DOH-naht
is there anything money can't buy?

A realistic, albeit cynical, observation of Horace, literally "money, like a queen, gives both rank and beauty." At least in the eyes of some. (See also NON DEFICIENTE CRUMENA.)

etiam capillus unus habet umbram suam
EH-tih-yahm kah-PIHL-luus OO-nuus HAH-beht UUM-brahm SUU-wahm
don't take anyone or anything for granted

Publilius Syrus telling us, in "even a single hair has its shadow," that we must give due attention to everyone and everything in our lives, no matter how apparently insignificant.

etiam perire ruinae
EH-tih-yahm peh-REE-reh ruu-WEE-nī
even the ruins have perished

A sad observation of Lucan, telling us humanity's past glories have disappeared. And the Romans did their part in destroying them.

etiam sanato vulnere cicatrix manet
EH-tih-yahm saah-NAAH-toh WUUL-neh-reh kih-KAAH-treeks MAH-neht
even when the wound has healed, the scar remains

And we never forget the wound—with or without professional assistance. (See also CICATRIX MANET.)

etiam si Cato dicat
EH-tih-yahm see KAH-toh DEE-kaht
even if Cato were to say it

Cato was a man of strict justice and blunt speech, so to his contemporaries anything he said was taken as true. The phrase *etiam si Cato dicat*, therefore, is used to express incredulity, as in "I wouldn't believe what you are telling me *etiam si Cato dicat.*"

etiam stultis acuit ingenium fames
EH-tih-yahm STUUL-tees AH-kuu-wiht ihn-GEH-nih-yuum FAH-mays
a potent motivator

This proverb, "hunger sharpens the wits even of fools," tells us that when hunger strikes, even dullards become resourceful. And when they do, who knows what desperate actions may ensue?

et modo quae fuerat semita facta via est

eht MAW-daw kwī FUU-weh-raht SAY-mih-tah FAHK-tah
WIH-yah ehst

next come the shopping malls

Martial, in writing that "and what had been only a footpath became a highway," looked happily on the changes wrought by advancing civilization. He never envisioned how things would turn out in the next millennia.

et qui nolunt occidere quemquam posse volunt

eht kwee NOH-luunt awk-KIH-deh-reh KWEHM-kwahm
PAWS-seh WAW-luunt

is this why crime stories dominate prime time?

Juvenal, observing the dark side of human nature, wrote "those who do not wish to kill anyone wish they were able."

et sceleratis sol oritur

eht skeh-leh-RAAH-tees sohl AW-rih-tuur

the sun shines even on the wicked

Seneca the Younger, providing the original model for a sixteenth-century English proverb, "the sun shines on all alike," meaning that nature treats all people the same or, in a modern interpretation, all people are created equal. What happens once the level playing field has had its chance is anyone's guess and the responsibility of each of us.

et semel emissum volat irrevocabile verbum

eht SEH-mehl ay-MEES-suum WAW-laht ihr-reh-waw-
KAAH-bih-leh WEHR-buum

watch what you say

Horace, who understood how nasty words can have consequences, cautioning us to be circumspect in our speech, literally "and a word once uttered flies away, never to be recalled."

eventus stultorum magister
ay-WEHN-tuus stuul-TOH-ruum mah-GIHS-tehr
fools can only learn through experience

Livy, telling us literally that "the result is the instructor of fools" and, by implication, there is no other way for fools to learn. (See also EMPTA DOLORE DOCET EXPERIENTIA.)

e vestigio
ay wehs-TEE-gih-yoh
instantly

ex abrupto
ehks ahb-RUUP-toh
out of the blue

Also translated as "without preliminaries" and, more literally, "abruptly."

ex abundante cautela
ehks ah-buun-DAHN-teh kow-TAY-laah
from excessive caution

Excessive caution can paralyze.

ex Africa semper aliquid novi
ehks AAH-frih-kaah SEHM-pehr AH-lih-kwihd NAW-wee
there is always something new out of Africa

This saying, an allusion to the ancient belief that Africa abounded in strange monsters, derives from a Greek proverb quoted by Pliny the Elder. Incidentally, to the ancients, Africa was a Roman province, now called Tunisia.

ex arena funiculum nectis
ehks ah-RAY-naah foo-NIH-kuu-luum NEHK-tihs
you're attempting the impossible

Literally "you're weaving a rope of sand." (See also ARENAE MANDAS SEMINA and ARENA SINE CALCE.)

exceptis excipiendis
ehks-KEHP-tees ehks-kih-pih-YEHN-dees
due exceptions being made

In generalizations we make, that is. Literally, "excepting what is to be excepted."

excerpta
ehks-KEHRP-tah
excerpts

Also translated as "extracts" and "selections."

ex commodo
ehks KAWM-maw-doh
conveniently *or* at one's convenience

ex confesso
ehks kohn-FEHS-soh
admittedly *or* confessedly

ex desuetudine amittuntur privilegia
ehks day-sway-TOO-dih-neh aah-miht-TUUN-tuur pree-wih-LAY-gih-yah
use it or lose it

A legal maxim, "by disuse are privileges lost."

exempla sunt odiosa
ehks-EHM-plah suunt oh-dih-YOH-sah
examples are odious

We are accustomed to hearing the fifteenth-century proverb "comparisons are odious," meaning that the drawing of analogies is offensive. Now we find as well that examples must be chosen with great care lest they also be seen as offensive.

exemplo plus quam ratione vivimus
ehks-EHM-ploh ploos kwahm rah-tih-YOH-neh WEE-wih-muus
do what I do, not what I say

A maxim, literally "we live more by example than by reason," suggesting that we are influenced less by moral precepts—taught usually by teachers, parents, or ministers—than by what we see these same people do.

ex eodem ore calidum et frigidum efflare
ehks eh-YOH-dehm OH-reh KAH-lih-duum eht FREE-gih-duum ehf-FLAAH-reh
to blow hot and cold from the same mouth

To give conflicting signals—a confusing and discouraging type of behavior.

exercitatio optimus est magister
ehks-ehr-kih-TAAH-tih-yoh AWP-tih-muus ehst mah-GIHS-tehr
practice is the best instructor

Or, as we are wont to say, practice makes perfect.

ex fide fortis
ehks FIH-day FAWR-tihs
strong through faith

ex granis fit acervus
ehks GRAAH-nees fiht ah-KEHR-wuus
Keogh plans plus IRAs—every bit helps

We all know—and who would deny?—that assiduity pays off in the end. The problem is that too many of us are unhappy with anything but an immediate payoff. The rest act in accordance with this proverb, literally "many grains make a heap," and put aside a little out of each paycheck. Sure enough, the savers do achieve financial independence in their retirement years—with the help of Social Security, that is.

ex imo corde
ehks EE-moh KAWR-deh
from the bottom of the heart

ex improviso
ehks ihm-proh-WEE-soh
suddenly *or* unexpectedly

ex natura rerum
ehks naah-TOO-raah RAY-ruum
from the nature of things

ex necessitate
ehks neh-kehs-sih-TAAH-teh
from necessity *or* necessarily

ex ore parvulorum veritas
ehks OH-reh pahr-wuu-LOH-ruum WAY-rih-taahs
out of the mouths of babes (comes) truth

So we should always listen to what children say.

ex oriente lux, ex occidente lex
ehks aw-rih-YEHN-teh looks ehks awk-kih-DEHN-teh layks
enlightenment from the East, our practical side from the West

Devotees of Eastern philosophy and religion will probably prefer the free rendering of *ex oriente lux, ex occidente lex* given above rather than its literal translation, "light (comes) out of the East, law from the West."

experientia docet
ehks-peh-rih-YEHN-tih-yah DAW-keht
we learn from experience

Literally "experience teaches." (See also USUS EST OPTIMUS MAGISTER and USUS TE PLURA DOCEBIT.)

experto crede

See CREDE EXPERTO.

expertus metuit
ehks-PEHR-tuus MEH-tuu-wiht
the experienced person is apprehensive

In propounding this wisdom, Horace had in mind the dangers inherent in cultivating the friendship of powerful people—be careful lest you get burned! So Horace is telling us that while we may think it wonderful to rub shoulders with the politically powerful, people who have been around the track a few times are always on guard and take pains to protect themselves.

explorant adversa viros
ehks-PLOH-rahnt ahd-WEHR-sah WIH-rohs
when the going gets tough, the tough get going

Literally "misfortunes put men to the test."

expressis verbis
ehks-PREHS-sees WEHR-bees
in so many words

Literally "in explicit terms."

ex scintilla incendium
ehks skihn-TIHL-laah ihn-KEHN-dih-yuum
from a spark a conflagration

A minor problem uncorrected can build and build and finally end in catastrophe—a two-bit break-in can eventually bring down a U.S. president. Going back a few centuries, we have the English proverb "for want of a nail the shoe was lost, for want of a shoe the horse was lost, for want of a horse the rider was lost . . ."

ex umbra in solem
ehks UUM-braah ihn SOH-lehm
from shade into sunlight

Our so-called sunshine laws exemplify *ex umbra in solem,* casting light on official government records and meetings by granting access previously denied to the public. (See also QUI MALE AGIT ODIT LUCEM.)

ex umbris et imaginibus in veritatem
ehks UUM-brees eht ih-maah-GIH-nih-buus ihn way-rih-TAAH-tehm
from shadows and apparitions to reality

This was the epitaph of Cardinal Newman (1801–1891), alluding to the soul's journey to God. (See COR AD COR LOQUITUR for his motto.)

ex vitio alterius sapiens emendat suum
ehks WIH-tih-yoh ahl-teh-REE-yuus SAH-pih-yayns ay-MEHN-daht SUU-wuum
learn from the mistakes of others

Publilius Syrus, telling us literally—and hopefully—"from another's fault, a wise person corrects his own." (See also EVENTUS STULTORUM MAGISTER, which tells us that fools do not learn anything from the mistakes of others.)

ex vitulo bos fit
ehks WIH-tuu-loh bohs fiht
from a calf comes an ox

This saying reminds us that small things in time can grow to impressive proportions. Nurture tender youth and be patient while it grows. (See also PARVIS E GLANDIBUS QUERCUS.)

F

faber est quisque fortunae suae
FAH-behr ehst KWIHS-kweh fawr-TOO-nī SUU-wī
everyone is the architect of his or her own success

Or failure, since *fortunae* can also be translated as "misfortune."

fac et excusa
fahk eht ehks-KOO-saah
make your move

Fac et excusa, which can stand as the motto of successful people—all of whom have surely had their shares of mistakes and failures—translates nearly literally as "do it and make excuses later." The worst thing one can do is habitually put off and put off and put off, whether because of uncertainty about the correctness of planned actions or because penalties for possible errors look too onerous.

facies tua computat annos
FAH-kih-yays TUU-wah kawm-POO-taht AHN-nohs
check the mirror, not the calendar

Juvenal telling all of us literally "your face keeps count of the years." Of course, today we have sunblock and plastic surgery for those who do not appreciate what they may see in their mirrors.

facile est inventis addere
FAH-kih-leh ehst ihn-WEHN-tees AHD-deh-reh
that's why editors were born

Literally "it's easy to add to things already invented." And, of course, it's hard to do anything original.

facile largiri de alieno
FAH-kih-leh lahr-GEE-ree day ah-lih-YAY-noh
sure, take the lawn mower

While most people think hard before lending their own possessions, they are often more amenable to lending things that don't belong to them. This must have been true during Roman times if we can judge from this proverb, literally "it's easy to be generous with another person's property."

facinus quos inquinat aequat
FAH-kih-nuus kwohs IHN-kwih-naht Ī-kwaht
a criminal is a criminal is a criminal

A maxim of Lucan, "crime levels those whom it contaminates," telling us that anyone guilty of a crime—no matter how petty—is still to be regarded as a criminal. Thus, white collars, blue collars, and blazer collars all stain.

facta sunt potentiora verbis
FAHK-tah suunt paw-tehn-tih-YOH-rah WEHR-bees
don't talk of love, show me!

This proverb, literally "deeds are more powerful than words," teaches that what we actually do makes a much greater impression than what we say. Everyone—from politicians to students with assignments due—who talks a good game but never gets around to accomplishing what he or she promises will quickly lose support and credibility and confirm the validity of *facta sunt potentiora verbis.*

fac ut sciam
fahk uut SKIH-yahm
don't leave me in the dark

Also translated as "tell me," and more literally as "make me be aware."

faex populi
fīks PAW-puu-lee
the rabble

Cicero's phrase for "the common people," literally "the dregs of the people." The bitterness intrinsic in the phrase becomes apparent when we relate *faex* and its plural *faeces* (FĪ-kays) to the English derivative "feces," which in Great Britain is spelled "faeces" and, like "feces," is pronounced FEE-seez. Enough said. (See also IGNOBILE VULGUS.)

fallacia alia aliam trudit
fahl-LAAH-kih-yah AH-lih-yah AH-lih-yahm TROO-diht
tell one lie, then another, and another . . .

A proverb of Terence, literally "one deceit presses hard upon another." Sir Walter Scott (1771–1832) said it more memorably:

> Oh, what a tangled web we weave,
> When first we practice to deceive!

(See also SCELERE VELANDUM EST SCELUS.)

fallaci nimium ne crede lucernae
fahl-LAAH-kee NIH-mih-yuum nay KRAY-deh luu-KEHR-nī
don't say you love her until you see her in daylight

Ovid, well aware of how flattering artificial light can be, gives practical advice to young men and old, literally "trust not too much to deceitful lamplight."

falsus in uno, falsus in omnibus
FAHL-suus ihn OO-noh FAHL-suus ihn AWM-nih-buus
your first slip robs you of your credibility

As every trial lawyer knows, an effective way to discredit testimony that may damage a case is to demonstrate to the jury that the witness has not been consistently truthful. Thus, *falsus in uno, falsus in omnibus,* "false in one thing, false in everything."

fama clamosa
FAAH-mah klaah-MOH-sah
the latest scandal

Literally "a noisy rumor."

fama nihil est celerius
FAAH-maah NIH-hihl ehst keh-LEH-rih-yuus
nothing is swifter than rumor

See also VIRES ACQUIRIT EUNDO.

fari quae sentiat
FAAH-ree kwī SEHN-tih-yaht
to say what one thinks

The mark of a bold person—not always esteemed by others.

fatigatis humus cubile est
fah-tee-GAAH-tees HUU-muus kuu-BEE-leh ehst
dead tired, you'll sleep anywhere

Literally "to the wearied the ground is a bed."

felicitas nutrix est iracundiae
fay-LEE-kih-taahs NOO-treeks ehst ee-raah-KUUN-dih-yī
nothing like a bit of good luck to pick up the spirits

This observation, literally "prosperity is the nurse of irascibility," tells us that even an inveterate grouch will brighten up when things go the right way.

ferae naturae
FEH-rī naah-TOO-rī
of an untamed nature

A legal term for an undomesticated animal or bird.

feriis caret necessitas
FAY-rih-yees KAAH-reht neh-KEHS-sih-taahs
necessity has no holidays

feriunt summos fulgura montes
FEH-rih-yuunt SUUM-mohs FUUL-guu-rah MAWN-tays
keep your powder dry and your head down

Our chances of attracting adverse criticism increase markedly when we achieve some prominence, according to this observation from Horace, literally "bolts of lightning strike the mountaintops." Most critics don't bother to attack the rest of us.

fervet opus
FEHR-weht AW-puus
I'm making progress

Virgil, reporting that a project is moving briskly forward, literally "the work glows."

fessus viator
FEHS-suus wih-YAAH-tawr
a weary traveler

festinatio tarda est
fehs-tee-NAAH-tih-yoh TAHR-dah ehst
more haste, less speed

Advice often given and often ignored, literally "haste is late."

fiat experimentum in corpore vili
FEE-yaht ehks-pehh-rih-MEHN-tuum ihn KAWR-paw-reh WEE-lee
don't experiment on things of value

Good advice, literally "let an experiment be made on a worthless body (or object)."

fidelis ad urnam
fih-DAY-lihs ahd UUR-nahm
true till death

Friendship or love can't ask for greater constancy, literally "faithful to the (funerary) urn."

fidem qui perdit nihil ultra perdere potest
FIH-dehm kwee PEHR-diht NIH-hihl OOL-traah PEHR-deh-reh PAW-tehst
above all, guard your credit rating

Publilius Syrus offering all entrepreneurs excellent advice, "he (or she) who loses credit can lose nothing further."

fide, sed cui vide
FEE-deh sehd koowee WIH-day
trust, but take care whom (you trust)

fides facit fidem
FIH-days FAH-kiht FIH-dehm
trust begets trust

Trust is a two-way street, according to this proverb, literally "faith creates faith."

fidus et audax
FEE-duus eht OW-daaks
faithful and bold

filius nullius
FEE-lih-yuus nool-LEE-yuus
a bastard

This term, literally "a son of nobody," is also given as **filius populi** (PAW-puu-lee), with the meaning "bastard" and translated literally as "a son of the people."

finis ecce laborum!
FEE-nihs EHK-keh lah-BOH-ruum
behold the end of our labors!

See also ERGO BIBAMUS!

flamma fumo est proxima
FLAHM-mah FOO-moh ehst PRAWKS-ih-mah
where there's smoke, there's fire

Plautus, telling us literally "flame is very close to fire," so if you smell smoke you had better believe that something is on fire. Likewise, if you suspect that skulduggery is afoot, you had better investigate.

flecti, non frangi
FLEHK-tee nohn FRAHN-gee
to bend, not to break

The motto of someone who is willing to accommodate change, but not willing to give up.

flos iuventutis (or juventutis)
flohs yuu-wehn-TOO-tihs
the flower of youth

forma bonum fragile est
FAWR-mah BAW-nuum FRAH-gih-leh ehst
beauty is a fleeting blessing

> Ovid, on the transitory nature of good looks. (See also FORMA
> FLOS, FAMA FLATUS.)

forma flos, fama flatus
FAWR-mah flohs FAAH-mah FLAAH-tuus
beauty is a flower, fame a breath

> And this compounds the despair inherent in FORMA BONUM
> FRAGILE EST.

forte scutum, salus ducum
FOHR-teh SKOO-tuum SAH-loos DUU-kuum
a strong shield is the safety of leaders

> Another argument for the efficacy of building armies rather
> than providing for the needs of ordinary people. This argument
> may be more true for despots than for leaders of enlightened
> democracies.

fortuna favet fatuis
fohr-TOO-nah FAH-weht FAH-tuu-wees
fortune favors fools

fortuna multis dat nimium, nulli satis
fohr-TOO-nah MUUL-tees daht NIH-mih-yuum NOOL-
lee SAH-tihs
no one ever is given too much

When gamblers win a trifecta, they fret at not having bet twice as much as they did. Martial makes this attitude clear in this adage, literally "to many fortune gives too much, to none enough."

fraus pia
frows PIH-yaḥ
a pious fraud

The worst kind. Also given as PIA FRAUS.

fructu non foliis arborem aestima
FROOK-too nohn FAW-lih-yees AHR-baw-rehm ĪS-tih-maah
judge by results, not by appearances

Phaedrus cautioning us to "judge a tree by its fruit, not by its leaves."

frustra laborat qui omnibus placere studet
FROOS-traah lah-BOH-raht kwee AWM-nih-buus plah-KAY-reh STUU-deht
you can't please the entire world

A proverb worthy of keeping in mind, literally "he labors in vain who strives to please everybody."

fugere est triumphus
FUU-geh-reh ehst trih-YUUM-phuus
to flee is a triumph

Under the appropriate circumstances. Consider the words of Shakespeare's Falstaff: "The better part of valor is discretion; in the which better part I have saved my life." And if you need a jingle to recite while you are fleeing, recall:

> He that fights and runs away
> Lives to fight another day.

furari litoris arenas
foo-RAAH-ree LEE-taw-rihs ah-RAY-naahs
to undertake a never-ending task

> Literally "to steal the sands of the seashore."

G

Gallia est omnis divisa in partes tres
GAHL-lih-yah ehst AWM-nihs dee-WEE-sah ihn PAHR-tays trays
all Gaul is divided into three parts

> The opening sentence of Julius Caesar's *Commentaries on the Gallic War*—once the start of every budding Latinist's long journey through the literature of ancient Rome.

gaudet tentamine virtus
GOW-deht tehn-TAAH-mih-neh WIHR-toos
always ready to be tested

> Literally "courage rejoices in trial." *Tentamine* is also given as **temptamine** (tehmp-TAAH-mih-neh), also meaning "in trial."

gens bracata
gayns braah-KAAH-tah
civilians

> In Roman times, when clothes really made the man, Gauls and barbarians dressed differently from Roman citizens. So the foreign folk were the *gens bracata*, literally "trousered people," while Roman citizens were **gens togata** (taw-GAAH-tah), literally "togaed people."

genus est mortis male vivere
GEH-nuus ehst MAWR-tihs MAH-lay WEE-weh-reh
behave yourself

> Good counsel from Ovid, "to live evilly is a kind of death."

gloria virtutis umbra
GLOH-rih-yah wihr-TOO-tihs UUM-brah
glory is the shadow of virtue

> The Romans made much of **virtus** (WIHR-toos), a word that has many meanings, including "strength," "bravery," "valor," and "excellence." (See, for example, the many entries beginning with VIRTUS.)

gradatim
grah-DAAH-tihm
gradually *or* step by step

> Thus the assertion **gradatim vincimus** (WIHN-kih-muus), freely translated as "we conquer by degrees." As long as we are patient, we need not overwhelm an adversary.

gradu diverso, via una
GRAH-doo dee-WEHR-soh WIH-yah OO-nah
pursuing the same goal, but with a different timetable

> This phrase, literally "with different pace, (but) on one road," comes in handy when, for example, two or more scientists, social reformers, or the like are working independently toward identical goals.

Graecia capta ferum victorem cepit
GRĪ-kih-ya KAHP-tah FEH-ruum week-TOH-rehm KAY-piht
captive Greece took captive its uncivilized victor

This from Horace, who understood what really matters once armed combat ends. While the Romans many times, but not always, defeated the Greeks, the Romans were well aware that Greek culture had made an indelible mark on Rome. So, in the end, the defeated Greeks were the real winners.

gratia gratiam parit
GRAAH-tih-yah GRAAH-tih-yahm PAH-riht
kindness begets kindness

Always? Let's hope so.

gratis dictum
GRAAH-tees DIHK-tuum
a mere assertion

Literally "a gratuitous statement," unsupported by evidence and so not to be taken as necessarily valid. For example, consider "we will not be undersold."

gratis pro Deo
GRAAH-tees proh DEH-yoh
free of cost

Literally "for God's sake."

grave delictum
GRAH-weh day-LEEK-tuum
a grave offense

graviora manent
grah-wih-YOH-rah MAH-nehnt
the worst is yet to come

A dire prediction from Virgil, "more grievous perils remain."

graviora quaedam sunt remedia periculis
grah-wih-YOH-rah KWĪ-dahm suunt reh-MEH-dih-yah
peh-REE-kuu-lees

maybe you ought to get a second opinion

Publilius Syrus telling us "some remedies are worse than
the dangers"—of a disease, that is. But we can surely apply
this observation to many proffered solutions to many perceived
problems.

gravis ira regum est semper
GRAH-wihs EE-rah RAY-guum ehst SEHM-pehr

the wrath of kings is always heavy

Seneca the Younger telling us not to fool around with kings
or other powerful persons or institutions.

gregatim
greh-GAAH-tihm

in crowds

But also translated as "in herds" and "in droves" and "in
flocks."

gutta cavat lapidem, consumitur anulus usu
GUUT-tah KAH-waht LAH-pih-dehm kohn-SOO-mih-
tuur AH-nuu-luus OO-soo

patience and persistence

This proverb, literally "a drop hollows out stone, a ring is
worn away by use," tells us that great things can be accomplished through continuing small efforts applied assiduously
over time.

H

habet et musca splenem
HAH-beht eht MUUS-kah SPLAY-nehm
even the least of us can be irritable

Literally "even a fly has its spleen." So be cautious in dealing with the weak.

hac urget lupus, hac canis
haahk UUR-geht LUU-puus haahk KAH-nihs
in deep trouble

Horace giving politicians and the rest of us a metaphor for any situation that appears to be hopeless, literally "on this side a wolf presses, on that a dog."

hae nugae seria ducent in mala
hī NOO-gī SAY-rih-yah DOO-kehnt ihn MAH-lah
stay clear of that slippery slope

Horace, in "these trifles will lead to serious evils," offering good counsel against committing even the slightest of moral, ethical, or professional missteps. (See also OMNE VITIUM IN PROCLIVI EST and PRINCIPIIS OBSTA.)

haec tibi dona fero
hīk TIH-bih DOH-nah FEH-roh
these gifts I bear to thee

Motto of Newfoundland.

haud passibus aequis
howd PAHS-sih-buus Ī-kwees
with unequal steps

Adapted from Virgil's **non passibus aequis** ("not with equal steps"), these words describe the slower progress of Aeneas's young son as he flees burning Troy with his father. Both are hurrying, but the child, whose stride is shorter, is unable to keep pace with his great father. This phrase may be effectively applied to anyone who attempts to follow in the footsteps of someone more accomplished. (See also SEQUITURQUE PATREM NON PASSIBUS AEQUIS.)

helluo librorum
HEHL-luu-woh lih-BROH-ruum
a bookworm

More literally "a devourer of books" or "a glutton for books."

heredem Deus facit, non homo
hay-RAY-dehm DEH-yuus FAH-kiht nohn HAW-moh
God makes the heir, not man

You never know how your children will turn out, no matter how conscientiously you raise them.

heu, vitam perdidi, operose nihil agendo
hehyoo WEE-tahm PEHR-dih-dee aw-peh-ROH-say NIH-hihl ah-GEHN-doh
I could have been a contender

A complaint occasionally and literally expressed as "alas, I have wasted my life, busily doing nothing."

hiatus valde deflendus
hih-YAY-tuus WAHL-day day-FLEHN-duus
long time no see

What do you say or write when you have put off for too long a call or a letter to an old friend? Here's a good phrase designed to get you off the hook, literally "a gap greatly to be lamented." Not to worry. Good friends will always forgive you.

hic funis nihil attraxit
hihk FOO-nihs NIH-hihl aht-TRAAHKS-iht
the scheme is a failure

"This line has taken no fish" or, more literally, "this line has attracted nothing." Apparently, ancient Romans were no different from Americans in thinking that suckers can fall for a line.

hic iacet (or jacet) lepus
heek YAH-keht LEH-puus
here's the problem

Literally "here lies the hare."

hinc lucem et pocula sacra
hihnk LOO-kehm eht POH-kuu-lah SAH-krah
from here (we receive) light and sacred libations

Motto of Cambridge University. For this I sent my children to college?

his non obstantibus
hees nohn awb-STAHN-tih-buus
notwithstanding these obstructions

historia vero testis temporum, lux veritatis
hihs-TAW-rih-yah WAY-roh TEHS-tihs TEHM-paw-ruum looks way-rih-TAAH-tihs
posterity will figure it all out

Valuable insight from Cicero, literally "history is indeed the witness of the times, the light of truth." But what about all those revisionists who rewrite or reinterpret history? They would say they've figured it all out. Historians continue to disagree.

hoc habet
hohk HAH-beht
he's had it

When Roman spectators at a gladiatorial contest—actually a fight to the death—yelled *hoc habet*, literally "he has it," they meant "he is hit," and a hit in such encounters meant the poor fellow would not live to fight again.

hoc sensu
hohk SAYN-soo
in this sense

hoc sustinete maius (or majus) ne veniat malum
hokk suus-tih-NAY-teh MAH-yuus nay WEH-nih-yaht MAH-luum
cop a plea

Advice from Phaedrus on the terrible things that befall humans, literally "endure this (evil) lest a greater evil (come upon you)."

hoc tempore
hohk TEHM-paw-reh
at this time

hominibus plenum, amicis vacuum
haw-MIH-nih-buus PLAY-nuum ah-MEE-kees WAH-kuu-wuum
a true friend is hard to find

Apparently even for Seneca the Younger, who said his world was literally "full of people, empty of friends."

homini ne fidas nisi cum quo modium salis absumpseris

HAW-mih-nee nay FEE-daahs NIH-sih kuum kwoh MAW-dih-yuum SAH-lihs ahb-SOOMP-seh-rees

take your time in judging people

Literally "trust no one except someone with whom you have consumed a peck of salt," a maxim that is down-to-earth, down-right up-to-date, and down on first impressions. When you consider that a peck is a quarter of a bushel, it would take dozens and dozens of highly seasoned power lunches to consume a peck of salt with anyone. By then, surely, you would be able to trust your judgment. (See also DECIPIT FRONS PRIMA MULTOS.)

hominis est errare, insipientis perseverare

HAW-mih-nihs ehst ehr-RAAH-reh een-sih-pih-YEHN-tihs pehr-seh-way-RAAH-reh

once is enough

This Roman proverb, "a person errs, a fool insists" adjures us not to make the same mistake twice.

homo homini aut deus aut lupus

HAW-moh HAW-mih-nee owt DEH-yuus owt LUU-puus

man is to man either a god or a wolf

Is there nothing in between?

homo multarum litterarum

HAW-moh muul-TAAH-ruum liht-teh-RAAH-ruum

a learned person

Also rendered as "a man of much learning" and literally as "a man of many letters." This phrase is not the source of the English phrase "man of letters," denoting an author or literary scholar.

homo nullius coloris
HAW-moh nool-LEE-yuus kaw-LOH-rihs

an uncertain quantity

This phrase, literally "a person of no color," can be used to indicate "a person of no political party," or more generally "a person whose opinions are unknown" or "an unknown person."

homo sui iuris (or juris)
HAW-moh SUU-wee YOO-rihs

an independent person

Literally "a person of his own law," in the sense that he is his own master, not subservient to others.

homo trium litterarum
HAW-moh TRIH-yuum liht-teh-RAAH-ruum

a thief

This phrase—a jocular allusion to HOMO MULTARUM LITTERARUM, "a person of many letters"—translates literally as "a person of three letters." And all Romans knew that the three letters were f-u-r, and **fur** (foor) in Latin means "thief."

honesta mors turpi vita potior
haw-NEHS-tah mawrs TUUR-pee WEE-taah PAW-tih-yawr

an honorable death is better than a disgraceful life

Tacitus, perhaps speaking for many of us.

honores mutant mores
haw-NOH-rays MOO-tahnt MOH-rays

honors alter character

Unfortunately, some people who rise to the top may forget how hard they struggled to achieve success and then do nothing to help those who are still struggling.

honos habet onus

HAW-nohs HAH-beht AW-nuus

honor carries responsibility

Literally "honor has its burden."

horae subsicivae

HOH-rī suub-sih-KEE-wī

free hours

Leisure time.

hos ego versiculos feci, tulit alter honores

hohs EH-gaw wehr-SIH-kuu-lohs FAY-kee TUU-liht AHL-tehr haw-NOH-rays

I wrote these insignificant lines of verse, another person took the credit

Virgil crying plagiarism.

hospes, hostis

HAWS-pehs HAWS-tihs

a stranger, an enemy

Expressing an attitude still prevalent in many cultures.

hostis honori invidia

HAWS-tihs haw-NOH-ree ihn-WIH-dih-yah

envy is the foe of esteem

humani nihil alienum
hoo-MAAH-nee NIH-hihl ah-lih-YAY-nuum
nothing human is foreign to me

A maxim adapted from Terence.

I

ibit eo quo vis qui zonam perdidit
EE-biht EH-yoh kwoh wees kwee ZOH-nahm PEHR-dih-diht
he who pays the piper calls the tune

Horace, who knew his way around, telling us literally that "he who has lost his money belt will go wherever you wish."

idem velle et idem nolle
IH-dehm WEHL-leh eht IH-dehm NOHL-leh
to like and dislike the same things

Kindred spirits in a happy relationship.

id facere laus est quod decet, non quod licet
ihd FAH-keh-reh lows ehst kwawd DEH-keht nohn kwawd LIH-keht
not merely legal, but also ethical

A proverb from Seneca the Younger, literally "he merits praise who does what he ought to do, not what he is allowed to do."

idoneus homo
ih-DOH-neh-yuus HAW-moh
a person of proven ability

Literally "a capable person."

ieiunus (or jejunus) raro stomachus vulgaria temnit
yay-YOO-nuus RAAH-roh STAW-mah-khuus wuul-
GAAH-rih-yah TEHM-niht
beggars can't be choosers

Horace, realistic as usual, telling us literally that "an empty stomach seldom scorns ordinary food."

ignavis semper feriae sunt
ihg-NAAH-wees SEHM-pehr FAY-rih-yī suunt
to the lazy, it's always holiday time

ignobile vulgus
ihg-NOH-bih-leh WUUL-guus
the rabble

Literally "the ignoble populace." Also translated as "the base-born multitude." (For an even more contemptuous term, see FAEX POPULI.)

ignoscito saepe alteri numquam tibi
ihg-NOHS-kih-toh SĪ-peh AHL-teh-ree NUUM-kwahm
TIH-bih
forgive others often, yourself never

ille crucem sceleris pretium tulit, hic diadema
IHL-leh KRUU-kehm SKEH-leh-rihs PREH-tih-yuum
TUU-liht hihk dih-yah-DAY-mah
the law does not treat all people fairly

Juvenal observing sardonically, "that man got the cross (cru-cifixion) as the reward for crime, this man a crown."

ille dolet vere qui sine teste dolet
IHL-leh DAW-leht WAY-ray kwee SIH-neh TEHS-teh
DAW-leht

true grief is private

We are told by Martial to distrust public displays of grief, literally "that person truly grieves who grieves without a witness."
Tell it to the staffs of TV news programs. Surely TV viewers can
grasp death or misfortune without being exposed to intrusive
close-ups of the faces of anguished families of the victims.

illotis manibus
ihl-LOH-tees MAH-nih-buus

unprepared

Literally "with unwashed hands."

imagines maiorum (or majorum)
ih-MAAH-gih-nays mah-YOH-ruum

portraits of ancestors

imitatores, servum pecus
ih-mih-taah-TOH-rays SEHR-wuum PEH-kuus

don't be a copycat

Imitation has been called the sincerest form of flattery, but
not by Horace, here venting his spleen on lesser writers who
preyed on him, addressing them literally as "you imitators, a
slavish herd." (See also O IMITATORES, SERVUM PECUS!)

impavidum ferient ruinae
ihm-PAH-wih-duum FEH-rih-yehnt ruu-WEE-nī

nothing can shatter the steadfastness of an upright man

Horace indulging in hyperbole on the character of a righ-
teous person, literally "the ruins (of the world) will strike him
undaunted."

imperat aut servit collecta pecunia cuique
IHM-peh-raht owt SEHR-wiht kawl-LAYK-tah peh-KOO-nih-yah KOOWEE-kweh
money amassed either rules or serves us

Horace warning us to maintain control over our wealth lest it control us.

implicite
ihm-PLIH-kih-tay
by implication

impos animi
IHM-paws AH-nih-mee
feeble-minded

Literally "not master over (one's) mind."

impotens sui
IHM-paw-tayns SUU-wee
lacking self-control

imprimatur
ihm-prih-MAAH-tuur
let it be printed

This is the term used by ecclesiastical authorities in granting permission for publication of a book, pamphlet, etc. It has been taken into English with the same pronunciation and the meaning of "official sanction by any authorized body," as in "the National Cancer Institutes refused to give the research paper its imprimatur."

imprimis
ihm-PREE-mees
in the first place

Also taken as "especially" and "first in order."

in aere piscari, in mare venari
ihn AAH-yeh-reh pihs-KAAH-ree ihn MAH-reh way-
NAAH-ree
to chase rainbows

This metaphor, literally "to fish in the air, to hunt in the sea," applies to any pursuit of an impossible dream.

in aqua scribis
ihn AH-kwaah SKREE-bihs
you are writing in water

A way of telling a person that he or she is wasting time on something that will not endure.

in arena aedificas
ihn ah-RAY-naah ī-DIH-fih-kaahs
building castles in the air

This phrase, literally "you're building on sand," is useful in dismissing an idea or plan that is perceived as being impracticable. (See also IN AERE PISCARI, IN MARE VENARI.)

in caducum parietem inclinare
ihn kah-DOO-kuum pah-RIH-yeh-tehm ihn-klee-NAAH-
reh
to lean against a falling wall

A metaphor for an action based on misplaced faith.

incredulus odi
ihn-KRAY-duu-luus OH-dee

being skeptical, I detest it

An example from Horace of the compactness of Latin, which makes it possible to say much in few words.

incudi reddere
ihn-KOO-dee REHD-deh-reh

to touch up *or* to revise

Horace, who understood that it takes more than one draft to knock out polished verse, gave us this metaphor, literally "to return to the anvil."

incurvat genus senectus
ihn-KUUR-waht GEH-nuus seh-NEHK-toos

old age bends the knee

With advancing years do the elderly become more submissive to the wishes of others than they were when they were in their prime? Maybe.

in Deo speramus
ihn DEH-yoh spay-RAAH-muus

in God we hope

Motto of Brown University.

indictum sit
ihn-DIHK-tuum siht

bite your tongue

Literally "let it be unsaid."

in diem vivere
ihn DIH-yehm WEE-weh-reh
to live from hand to mouth

Literally "to live for today," telling us that when we scarcely have enough to get by on even for one day, there's no point in discussing retirement plans.

inedita
ihn-AY-dih-tah
unpublished works

A bibliographic term.

inest sua gratia parvis
IHN-ehst SUU-wah GRAAH-tih-yah PAHR-wees
even little things have a charm of their own

in fine
ihn FEE-neh
in the end

The origin of the English expression "in fine" (fīn), meaning "briefly" or "in short."

ingens telum necessitas
IHN-gayns TAY-luum neh-KEHS-sih-taahs
necessity is the mother of invention

Literally "necessity is a powerful weapon." (For a second phrase meaning "necessity is the mother of invention," see NE-CESSITAS RATIONUM INVENTRIX.)

iniquum petas ut aequum feras
ihn-EE-kwuum PEH-taahs uut Ī-kwuum FEH-raahs
the gentle art of haggling

Insurance lawyers and literary agents surely have learned this Latin phrase, literally "ask for what is unreasonable so that you may obtain what is just."

in nihilum nil posse reverti
ihn NIH-hih-luum neel PAWS-seh reh-WEHR-tee
matter is indestructible

The perception by Persius that literally "there is nothing that can be reduced to nothing."

in nocte consilium
ihn NAWK-teh kohn-SIH-lih-yuum
the night brings counsel

Or, as we would say idiomatically, "it's best to sleep on the matter."

in nuce
ihn NUU-keh
in a nutshell

in oculis civium
ihn AW-kuu-lees KEE-wih-yuum
in public

Literally "in the eyes of citizens."

inops, potentem dum vult imitari, perit
IHN-awps paw-TEHN-tehm duum wuult ih-mih-TAAH-ree PEH-riht
don't spend beyond your means

Phaedrus telling us literally "a poor man perishes when he tries to imitate a powerful man."

in pace leones, in proelio cervi
ihn PAAH-keh leh-YOH-nays ihn PROY-lih-yoh KEHR-wee

it's easy to talk a good game

Blustering patriots who advocate war but change their mind when conflict is imminent may be characterized as here, literally "lions in peace, deer in battle."

in poculis
ihn POH-kuu-lees

while drinking

Literally "in (one's) cups." Of course, when we say in English that a person is "in his cups," we are indicating that he is drunk, and *in poculis* may be interpreted in the same way.

in proverbium cessit, sapientiam vino adumbrari
ihn proh-WEHR-bih-yuum KEHS-siht sah-pih-YEHN-tih-yahm WEE-noh ah-duum-BRAAH-ree

don't take up serious matters when you drink

This is Pliny the Elder telling us literally "it has become a proverb that wisdom is obscured by wine."

in silvam ligna ferre
ihn SIHL-wahm LIHG-nah FEHR-reh

to carry coals to Newcastle

Literally "to carry wood to the forest." (See also PISCEM NATARE DOCES.)

integra mens augustissima possessio
IHN-teh-grah mayns ow-guus-TIHS-sih-mah paws-SEHS-sih-yoh

a sound mind is the most majestic possession

in tenebris
ihn TEH-neh-brees

in a state of doubt

> Literally "in darkness."

inter canem et lupum
IHN-tehr KAH-nehm eht LUU-puum

twilight

> This phrase, literally "between a dog and a wolf," also means "between two difficulties" as well as "twilight." (See also HAC URGET LUPUS, HAC CANIS.)

interdum stultus opportuna loquitur
ihn-TEHR-duum STUUL-tuus awp-pawr-TOO-nah LAW-kwih-tuur

sometimes (even) a fool says something useful

intra parietes
IHN-traah pah-RIH-yeh-tays

within the walls (of a house or other building)

> The principal reason for including this phrase is to call attention to the Latin noun **paries** (PAH-rih-yays), meaning "wall," and so shed light on the English phrase "parietal rules"—we also think of them as "house rules."

intra verba peccare
IHN-traah WEHR-bah pehk-KAAH-reh

to offend in words only

> Not in actions, that is.

invictus maneo

ihn-WEEK-tuus MAH-neh-yoh

I remain unconquered *or* I remain unbeaten.

This pertains to an unconquered male. An unconquered female would say **invicta** (ihn-WEEK-tah) **maneo**.

invidia gloriae comes

ihn-WIH-dih-yah GLOH-rih-yī KAW-mehs

envy is glory's companion

Too often true.

in vota miseros ultimus cogit timor

ihn WOH-tah MIH-seh-rohs OOL-tih-muus KOH-giht TIH-mawr

there are no atheists in foxholes

Nor were there in ancient Rome, according to Seneca, who told us "fear of death drives the wretched to make vows to the gods."

irritabis crabrones

ihr-ree-TAAH-bihs kraah-BROH-nays

you will stir up the hornets

A warning from Plautus to beware of those who have the capacity to sting.

iudex (or judex) damnatur cum nocens absolvitur

YOO-dehks DAHM-naah-tuur kuum NAW-kayns ahb-SAWL-wih-tuur

the judge is condemned when a criminal is set free

Publilius Syrus giving us his notion of where the blame lies when we disagree with a verdict.

iure (or jure) divino
YOO-reh dee-WEE-noh
by divine right *or* by divine law

ius (or jus) gentium
yoos GEHN-tih-yuum
international law

> Literally "the law of nations."

ius (or jus) naturale
yoos naah-too-RAAH-leh
natural law

ius (or jus) scriptum
yoos SKREEP-tuum
written law

J

jejunus raro stomachus vulgaria temnit

> See IEIUNUS RARO STOMACHUS VULGARIA TEMNIT.

judex damnatur cum nocens absolvitur

> See IUDEX DAMNATUR CUM NOCENS ABSOLVITUR.

jure divino

See IURE DIVINO.

jus gentium

See IUS GENTIUM.

jus naturale

See IUS NATURALE.

jus scriptum

See IUS SCRIPTUM.

L

labor ipse voluptas
LAH-bawr IHP-seh waw-LUUP-taahs
labor itself is pleasure

For people who love their work, at least.

laborum dulce lenimen
lah-BOH-ruum DUUL-keh lay-NEE-mehn
sweet solace of my toils

Horace, addressing his lyre, gives us a saccharine phrase to use when turning to a pet dog, a crossword puzzle, a violin, or the like while taking a break from a demanding intellectual or creative project.

lacrimis oculos suffusa nitentis

LAH-krih-mees AW-kuu-lohs suuf-FOO-sah nih-TEHN-
tees

her sparkling eyes bedewed with tears

A lovely image from Virgil.

lapis philosophorum

LAH-pihs phih-law-saw-PHOH-ruum

the philosopher's stone

This is the hypothetical substance sought by ancient alche-
mists in the expectation that it would enable them to convert
base metals into gold.

Latine dictum

lah-TEE-nay DIHK-tuum

spoken in Latin

lato sensu

LAAH-toh SAYN-soo

in a broad sense

The opposite of STRICTO SENSU.

latrante uno, latrat statim et alter canis

laah-TRAHN-teh OO-noh LAAH-traht STAH-tihm eht
AHL-tehr KAH-nihs

everybody wants to get into the act

The thought expressed literally here is that "when one dog
barks, another dog immediately barks." But the point of the adage is that when a basketball celebrity, for example, endorses
a particular kind of sneakers, suddenly kids in schoolyards and
playgrounds everywhere are all sporting the same sneakers.

laudari a viro laudato
low-DAAH-ree aah WIH-roh low-DAAH-toh
to be praised by someone who is himself praised

Far better than being praised by someone who has no standing.

laudumque immensa cupido
low-DUUM-kweh ihm-MAYN-sah kuu-PEE-doh
and a boundless desire for praise

Virgil being critical of those who have a passion for renown.

laus propria sordet
lows PRAW-prih-yah SAWR-deht
self-praise is debasing

legant prius et postea despiciant
LEH-gahnt PRIH-yuus eht PAWS-teh-yaah day-SPIH-kih-yahnt
but you haven't even read the book

The writer's lament upon receiving poor reviews, literally "let them read first and despise afterward."

legenda
leh-GEHN-dah
things to be read

leges mori serviunt
LAY-gays MOH-ree SEHR-wih-yuunt
laws are subservient to custom

Suggesting that good laws are based on actual practices, not on grand philosophic ideas.

leone fortior fides
leh-YOH-neh FAWR-tih-yawr FIH-days
faith is stronger than a lion

> After a manner of speaking.

leve fit quod bene fertur onus
LEH-weh fiht kwawd BEH-neh FEHR-tuur AW-nuus
enjoy your work

> Ovid telling us that "a load cheerfully borne becomes light."

lex uno ore omnes alloquitur
layks OO-noh OH-reh AWM-nays ahl-LAW-kwih-tuur
everyone is equal before the law

> Literally "the law speaks with one mouth to all." At least we hope it does.

liberavi animam meam
lee-beh-RAAH-wee AH-nih-mahm MEH-yahm
now it's off my mind

> Literally "I have freed my mind" or "I am relieved." Useful for anyone who confesses guilt or complicity in an illicit plot, extramarital affair, or the like. See also ABSOLVI MEAM ANIMAM.

libertas est potestas faciendi id quod iure (or jure) licet
lee-BEHR-taahs ehst paw-TEHS-taahs fah-kih-YEHN-dee ihd kwawd YOO-reh LIH-keht
liberty is the power of doing what is permitted by law

limae labor et mora
LEE-mī LAH-bawr eht MAW-rah
no wonder writers never meet their deadlines

Horace writing literally of "the toil and delay of revision," by which a literary work is brought to its final, polished state. The noun **lima** (LEE-mah) translates as "revision" when used figuratively, and as the tool called a "file" when used literally, so with a bit of imagination we envision serious writers applying files to their sentences in order to give them cutting edges.

limbus fatuorum
LIHM-buus fah-tuu-WOH-ruum
fools' paradise

The word *limbus*, literally a border or an edge, comes into English as *limbo*, a theological term for a celestial holding pen located on the edge of heaven for souls not fit to live among saints or sinners. Since intention is a requirement for sin, fools who commit evil are technically blameless and are shipped off to fools' paradise when they die.

lis litem generat
lees LEE-tehm GEH-neh-raht
You started it! No, you did!

Anyone who knows anything at all about the vicissitudes of domestic life knows literally that "strife begets strife." So what is one to do? Just remember that *lis* and *litem* can also be translated as "lawsuit"—the first in the nominative case, the second in the accusative—and both suggesting imminent deep and continuing trouble. Better nip disagreements in the bud. (For an example of how little disputes can grow, see MAXIMA BELLA EX LEVISSIMIS CAUSIS.)

lis litem resolvere
lees LEE-tehm reh-SAWL-weh-reh
to explain one obscurity by another

This phrase literally translates as "strife to settle strife," more broadly as "to resolve one dispute by introducing another." The end result of any of the three interpretations given here is that the parties to the dispute are no closer to a true resolution than when the process began. Now who would indulge in such folly? Nobody except for thousands of academics, economists, government officials, theologians, Internal Revenue code writers, and a few others.

litterae scriptae manet
LIHT-teh-rī SKREEP-tī MAH-neht
don't put it in writing

A warning, literally "the written words endure." And that goes for e-mails and text messages too. If the Romans had been more advanced in technology, they would also have cautioned against tape and video recorders.

litterae sine moribus vanae
LIHT-teh-rī SIH-neh MOH-rih-buus WAAH-nī
scholarship without morals is useless

Motto of the University of Pennsylvania.

longe absit!
LAWN-gay AHB-siht
God forbid!

Literally "far be it (from me)!"

longo sed proximus intervallo
LAWN-goh sehd PRAWKS-ih-muus ihn-tehr-WAHL-loh
a poor second

Virgil's phrase, literally "the next but separated by a great distance," for anyone or anything that doesn't even come close in a competition. Recall any horse losing a race to Secretariat.

luce lucet aliena
LOO-keh LOO-keht ah-lih-YAY-naah
any way you slice it, it's still plagiarism

> Literally "it shines with another's light."

lucri bonus est odor
LUU-kree BAW-nuus ehst AW-dawr
sweet is the odor of wealth

> A maxim from Juvenal. Notwithstanding the approval of Juvenal, we too often speak of "filthy lucre," a cliché employing an English word deriving from *lucrum*, the nominative form of *lucri*, meaning "wealth." (See also ODOR LUCRI.)

ludere cum sacris
LOO-deh-reh kuum SAH-krees
to trifle with sacred things

lumen naturale
LOO-mehn naah-too-RAAH-leh
natural intelligence

> Literally "the light of nature," but also translated as "enlightenment."

lumenque iuventae (or juventae) purpureum
loo-MEHN-kweh yuu-WEHN-tī puur-PUUR-eh-yuum
the radiant bloom of youth

> Literally "the purple light of youth." This is Virgil waxing eloquent about the prime of life—as it was seen back in ancient Rome.

lumen soli mutuum das
LOO-mehn SOH-lee MOO-tuu-wuum daahs
you're the top

Extravagant praise, literally "you lend light to the sun."

lupa
LUU-pah
she-wolf

But also "prostitute," leading to **lupanar** (luu-PAAH-nahr), meaning "brothel."

lux in tenebris
looks ihn TEH-neh-brees
light in the darkness

lux mundi
looks MUUN-dee
light of the world

Jesus Christ.

M

magister caerimoniarum
mah-GIHS-tehr kī-rih-moh-nih-YAAH-ruum
master of ceremonies

See also REX CONVIVII.

magna civitas, magna solitudo
MAHG-nah KEE-wih-taahs MAHG-nah soh-lih-TOO-doh
a great place to visit

In this adage, literally "a great city is a great desert," the noun *solitudo* is rendered as "desert," but it may also be taken as "loneliness."

magnae fortunae pericula

MAHG-nī fohr-TOO-nī peh-REE-kuu-lah

the dangers of great success

Tacitus gave us this phrase, and we substantiate it. Think of what has happened to so many of our sports superstars and financial wizards.

magnae spes altera Romae

MAHG-nī spays AHL-teh-rah ROH-mī

he's a real comer

Virgil's phrase, literally "a second hope of mighty Rome," was originally said of the son of Aeneas—considered by Romans to be the founder of their nation—but it can be said of any promising young person.

magna est vis consuetudinis

MAHG-nah ehst wees kohn-sway-TOO-dih-nihs

great is the power of habit

To provide good and not so good results.

magna servitus est magna fortuna

MAHG-nah SEHR-wih-toos ehst MAHG-nah fohr-TOO-nah

a great fortune is a great slavery

Seneca the Younger warning that wealth is not an unmixed blessing. (See what Tacitus said about this in MAGNAE FORTUNAE PERICULA.)

magnas inter opes inops
MAHG-naahs IHN-tehr AW-pays IHN-awps
poor amid great riches

Horace reminding us that general wealth in a society does not mean that everybody shares in it. So much for trickle-down economics.

magna vis est conscientiae
MAHG-nah wees ehst kohn-skih-YEHN-tih-yī
great is the power of conscience

magno conatu magnas nugas
MAHG-noh koh-NAAH-too MAHG-naahs NOO-gaahs
molehills from mountains

Terence, aware of how much time people waste on doing things that do not matter, pungently characterized this failing as "by great effort (to obtain) great trifles."

magnum vectigal est parsimonia
MAHG-nuum wayk-TEE-gahl ehst pahr-sih-MOH-nih-yah
save money by not wasting money

Cicero, apparently expert in the art of living on a budget, tells us literally "frugality is a great income."

magnus Alexander corpore parvus erat
MAHG-nuus ah-lehks-AHN-dehr KAWR-paw-reh PAHR-wuus EH-raht
you don't have to be seven feet tall

Literally "great Alexander was small of body." Alexander who? Alexander the Great (356–323 B.C.), the general who succeeded so well in building his empire that he became the model for many later imperialists.

maiores (or majores) pinnas nido extendisse
mah-YOH-rays PIHN-naahs NEE-doh ehks-tehn-DIHS-seh

to try to do better than one's parents

Horace, in an avian metaphor, "to have spread wings greater than the nest," that is, to soar above the status to which one was born. Apparently, Americans did not invent the American dream.

maiori (or majori) cedo
mah-YOH-ree KAY-doh

I yield to a superior

A gracious way to show deference or admit defeat. (See also CONCEDO.)

malam rem cum velis honestatem, improbes
MAH-lahm rehm kuum WEH-lees haw-nehs-TAAH-tehm IHM-praw-bays

a book banned in Boston will surely succeed

Publilius Syrus warning against providing publicity for ideas you oppose, "when you wish a bad thing to become something respectable, condemn it." Publilius would have made a first-class public relations expert.

male imperando summum imperium amittitur
MAH-lay ihm-peh-RAHN-doh SUU-muum ihm-PEH-rih-yuum aah-MIHT-tih-tuur

through misrule the greatest power can be lost

Publilius Syrus, this time offering political advice. (See also MALAM REM CUM VELIS HONESTATEM, IMPROBES.)

male narrando fabula depravatur
MAH-lay nahr-RAHN-doh FAAH-buu-lah day-prah-WAAH-tuur

a story is spoiled by bad telling

> Watch the timing and don't forget the punch line.

male parta, male dilabuntur
MAH-lay PAHR-tah MAH-lay dee-laah-BUUN-tuur

easy come, easy go

> Literally "things ill gained are ill lost."

malignum spernere vulgus
mah-LEEG-nuum SPEHR-neh-reh WUUL-guus

to scorn the ill-natured crowd

mali principii malus finis
MAH-lee preen-KIH-pih-yee MAH-luus FEE-nihs

from a bad beginning a bad ending

> For a related observation, see BONI PRINCIPII FINIS BONUS.

malo mori quam foedari
MAAH-loh MAW-ree kwahm foy-DAAH-ree

death before dishonor

> Literally "I had rather die than be disgraced."

malum est consilium quod mutari non potest
MAH-luum ehst kohn-SIH-lih-yuum kwawd moo-TAAH-ree nohn PAW-tehst

stay loose

> Publilius Syrus offering a slogan for pragmatists, literally "it is a bad plan that cannot be changed."

malum quia prohibitum
MAH-luum KWIH-yah praw-HIH-bih-tuum
an action wrong because it is prohibited

Not because it is immoral.

malum vas non frangitur
MAH-luum waahs nohn FRAHN-gih-tuur
a worthless dish doesn't break.

Only the expensive ones.

malus animus
MAH-luus AH-nih-muus
evil intent

malus pudor
MAH-luus PUU-dawr
false modesty

manu forti
MAH-noo FAWR-tee
forcible entry

A legal term, literally "with a strong hand."

manu militari
MAH-noo mee-lih-TAAH-ree
by armed force

Literally "by the military hand."

manus e nubibus
MAH-nuus ay NOO-bih-buus

a lucky break

> Literally "a hand from the clouds."

manus manum lavat
MAH-nuus MAH-nuum LAH-waht

one hand washes the other

> You help me, I help you.

marginalia
mahr-gih-NAAH-lih-yah

marginal notes

> Also "peripheral things."

Mars gravior sub pace latet
maahrs GRAH-wih-yawr suub PAAH-keh LAH-teht

the devil is in the details

> Literally "a more serious war lies hidden in the peace," in the peace treaty, that is.

mater artium necessitas
MAAH-tehr AHR-tih-yuum neh-KEHS-sih-taahs

necessity is the mother of the arts

> Another way of saying "necessity is the mother of invention." (See also INGENS TELUM NECESSITAS.)

maxima bella ex levissimis causis
MAHKS-ih-mah BEHL-lah ehks leh-WIHS-sih-mees KOW-sees

the greatest wars arise from very slight causes

Or, as we say, "one thing leads to another." (See also LIS LITEM GENERAT.)

maxima debetur puero reverentia

MAHKS-ih-mah day-BAY-tuur PUU-weh-roh reh-weh-REHN-tih-yah

the greatest respect is due a child

Juvenal said this, and many of us have been repeating it ever since.

maximum remedium irae mora est

MAHKS-ih-muum reh-MEH-dih-yuum EE-rī MAW-rah ehst

take time to cool off

Seneca the Younger counseling that "the greatest remedy for anger is delay." Shout it from the rooftops.

maximus in minimis

MAHKS-ih-muus ihn MIH-nih-mees

very great in very small things

Motto of a nitpicker.

mea virtute me involvo

MEH-yaah wihr-TOO-teh may ihn-WAWL-woh

I wrap myself up in my virtue

Horace, like so many of his contemporaries, saw virtue as redeeming. Rush Limbaugh, are you listening? (See, for example, DOMAT OMNIA VIRTUS.)

medicus curat, natura sanat

MEH-dih-kuus KOO-raht naah-TOO-rah SAAH-naht

the physician treats, nature cures

medium tenuere beati
MEH-dih-yuum teh-nuu-WAY-reh beh-YAAH-tee
happy are they who have kept a middle course

> Counsel for those who don't go too far to the left or right.

melioribus annis
meh-lih-YOH-rih-buus AHN-nees
in happier times

> A phrase from Virgil, literally "in the better years."

memorabilia
meh-moh-raah-BIH-lih-yah
things worth remembering

> Giving us the English word "memorabilia," pronounced meh-mawr-ə-BIH-lee-ə.

mens divinior
mayns dee-WEE-nih-yawr
an inspired soul

> A phrase from Horace, literally "a mind of diviner cast."

mens et manus
mayns eht MAH-nuus
mind and hand

> Motto of the Massachusetts Institute of Technology.

mens regnum bona possidet
mayns RAYG-nuum BAW-nah PAWS-sih-deht
a good mind possesses a kingdom

> Seneca the Younger on intelligence, first inherited and then applied to important matters.

mens sibi conscia recti
mayns SIH-bih KOHN-skih-yah RAYK-tee
a clear conscience

Virgil's phrase, literally and awkwardly "a mind aware within itself of rectitude."

mentiri splendide
mehn-TEE-ree SPLEHN-dih-day
to deceive magnificently

Also translated as "to lie magnificently."

mentis gratissimus error
MEHN-tihs graah-TIHS-sih-muus EHR-rawr
a most delightful hallucination

A phrase from Horace.

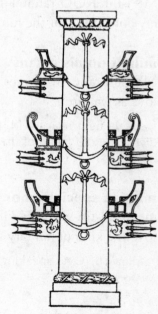

meo periculo
MEH-yoh peh-REE-kuu-loh
at my own risk

meo voto
MEH-yoh WOH-toh
by my wish

meret qui laborat
MEH-reht kwee lah-BOH-raht
hard work commands respect

Literally "he is deserving who is industrious."

merum sal
MEH-ruum saahl
genuine wit

Literally "pure salt." (See also SAL SAPIT OMNIA.)

meum et tuum
MEH-yuum eht TUU-wuum
mine and thine

A phrase used in law to characterize property held jointly by a couple. "The car is yours, the refrigerator is mine, and these chairs are *meum et tuum*."

mihi cura futuri
MIH-hih KOO-rah fuu-TOO-ree
my concern is for the future

militat omnis amans
MEE-lih-taht AWM-nihs AH-maahns
love as warfare

A thought from Ovid, literally "every lover serves as a soldier." The old battle of the sexes. (See also MILITIAE SPECIES AMOR EST.)

militiae species amor est
mee-LIH-tih-yī SPEH-kih-yays AH-mawr ehst
love is a kind of military service

Realistic Ovid speaking again of love. (See also MILITAT OMNIS AMANS.)

mirum in modum
MEE-ruum ihn MAW-duum
surprisingly

Caesar's phrase, literally "in a wonderful manner."

mitis sapientia
MEE-tihs sah-pih-YEHN-tih-yah
ripe wisdom *or* mellow wisdom

mole ruit sua
MOH-leh RUU-wiht SUU-waah
it is crushed by its own weight

A phrase from Horace, literally "it falls down of its own bulk." Useful for characterizing any overly complex argument, proposal, piece of legislation, plan, or the like.

monstrum horrendum, informe, ingens
MOHN-struum hawr-REHN-duum een-FAWR-meh IHN-gayns
a monster horrible, misshapen, huge

A chilling phrase from Virgil.

more maiorum (or majorum)
MOH-reh mah-YOH-ruum
traditionally

Literally "in the manner of one's ancestors."

more probato
MOH-reh praw-BAAH-toh
in the approved manner

mors ianua (or janua) vitae
mawrs YAAH-nuu-wah WEE-tī
the end is just the beginning

Literally "death is the gate of life." (See, for contrast, MORS ULTIMA LINEA RERUM EST.)

mors omnibus communis
mawrs AWM-nih-buus kawm-MOO-nihs
death is common to all

Who can deny it?

mors ultima linea rerum est
mawrs OOL-tih-mah LEE-neh-yah RAY-ruum ehst
death is the final boundary of things

mors ultima ratio
mawrs OOL-tih-mah RAH-tih-yoh
death is the final reckoning

mortuo leoni et lepores insultant
MAWR-tuu-woh leh-YOH-nee eht LEH-paw-rays een-
SUUL-tahnt
even hares leap upon (*or* insult) a dead lion

This animal metaphor tells us that when a powerful leader is
rendered ineffectual, even his most easily frightened opponent
can muster the courage to attack him.

motu proprio
MOH-too PRAW-prih-yoh
of one's own accord *or* impulse

mulier cum sola cogitat male cogitat
MUU-lih-yehr kuum SOH-lah KOH-gih-taht MAH-lay
KOH-gih-taht
beware a thoughtful woman

An ill-natured observation from Publilius Syrus, literally
"when a woman thinks alone she is plotting mischief."

mulier cupido quod dicit amanti in vento et rapida scribere oportet aqua

MUU-lih-yehr kuu-PEE-doh kwawd DEE-kiht ah-MAHN-tee ihn WEHN-toh eht RAH-pih-daah SKREE-beh-reh aw-PAWR-teht AH-kwaah

what a woman says to an ardent lover should be written on wind and running water

Catullus telling us that under demanding circumstances women do not always say precisely what they mean. Nor do men, one might hasten to add.

multa cadunt inter calicem supremaque labra

MUUL-tah KAH-duunt IHN-tehr KAH-lih-kehm suu-PRAY-mah-kweh LAH-brah

things can go wrong at the last moment

More literally "much falls between cup and lip" or, as we commonly say, "there's many a slip 'twixt the cup and the lip."

multa docet fames

MUUL-tah DAW-keht FAH-mays

hunger teaches us many things

For a more extravagant claim, see also ETIAM STULTIS ACUIT INGENIUM FAMES.

multa petentibus desunt multa

MUUL-tah peh-TEHN-tih-buus DAY-suunt MUUL-tah

to those who seek many things, many things are lacking

Horace telling us that those who covet much, are missing much.

multis utile bellum
MUUL-tees OO-tih-leh BEHL-luum

war profiteering is nothing new

Lucan telling us literally "war is profitable for many," indicating that profiteering went on even in ancient Rome.

multorum manibus magnum levatur onus
muul-TOH-ruum MAH-nih-buus MAHG-nuum leh-WAAH-tuur AW-nuus

many hands make light work

Literally "by the hands of many a great load is lightened." As long as all the hands don't think they are in charge of the operation. Recall the English proverb "too many cooks spoil the broth."

multum demissus homo
MUUL-tuum day-MEES-suus HAW-moh

a modest *or* unassuming man

A phrase from Horace.

munus Apolline dignum
MOO-nuus ah-PAWL-lih-neh DIHG-nuum

a gift worthy of Apollo

A phrase from Horace available for use in a thank-you note.

murus aeneus conscientia sana
MOO-ruus ah-YAY-neh-yuus kohn-skih-YEHN-tih-yah SAAH-nah

a sound conscience is a wall of brass

Shakespeare said it even better when he called a quiet conscience "a peace above all earthly dignities."

muscae volitantes
MUUS-kī waw-lih-TAHN-tays
floaters

A medical term. *Muscae volitantes,* literally "flying flies," may be spoken of in the physician's office. Commonly called "floaters," they are the moving specks many people see in their fields of vision.

mus non uni fidit antro
moos nohn OO-nee FEE-diht AHN-troh
a wise person always has a backup plan

A lesson for all of us from a little creature, literally "a mouse does not put its trust in one hole."

mutanda
moo-TAHN-dah
things to be altered

Commonly encountered in the phrase **mutatis mutandis** (moo-TAAH-tees moo-TAHN-dees), literally "things having been changed that had to be changed," and freely translated as "after making the necessary changes."

mutuus consensus
MOO-tuu-wuus kohn-SAYN-suus
mutual consent

N

nam tua res agitur paries cum proximus ardet
nahm TUU-wah rays AH-gih-tuur PAH-rih-yays kuum PRAWKS-ih-muus AHR-deht
ask not for whom the bell tolls

Horace telling us literally, "when your neighbor's house is on fire, you are in danger yourself."

natale solum
naah-TAAH-leh SAW-luum
native soil

> One's native country.

nati natorum et qui nascentur ab illis
NAAH-tee naah-TOH-ruum eht kwee naahs-KEHN-tuur ahb IHL-lees
children's children and those descended from them

> Virgil giving us an expressive phrase to think of when planning policies that may affect the future.

natio comoeda est
NAAH-tih-yoh koh-MOY-dah ehst
it is a nation of comic actors

> Juvenal speaking of the Greeks, whom he saw as decadent.

natura abhorret a vacuo
naah-TOO-rah ahb-HAWR-reht aah WAH-kuu-woh
nature abhors a vacuum

> An observation advanced by Descartes.

natus ad gloriam
NAAH-tuus ahd GLOH-rih-yahm
born to glory

natus nemo
NAAH-tuus NAY-moh
a nobody

Literally "born a nobody," a phrase from Plautus.

naufragium in portu facere
now-FRAH-gih-yuum ihn PAWR-too FAH-keh-reh
to snatch defeat from the jaws of victory

This apt nautical metaphor, "to shipwreck in port," may be used to describe the action of anyone who manages to fail when on the verge of success. (See also NAUFRAGIUM SIBI QUISQUE FACIT.)

naufragium sibi quisque facit
now-FRAH-gih-yuum SIH-bih KWIHS-kweh FAH-kiht
"The fault, dear Brutus, is not in our stars,
But in ourselves . . ."

Lucan, employing a nautical metaphor, tells us we have only ourselves to blame, literally "each man makes his own shipwreck." Did Shakespeare say it better? (See also NAUFRAGIUM IN PORTU FACERE.)

nec amor nec tussis celatur
nehk AH-mawr nehk TUUS-sihs kay-LAAH-tuur
neither love nor a cough can be hidden

For the same thought, see AMOR TUSSISQUE NON CELANTUR.

nec aspera terrent
nehk AHS-peh-rah TEHR-rehnt
we shall overcome

Literally "not even hardships deter us."

nec caput nec pedes

nehk KAH-puut nehk PEH-days

in confusion

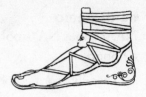

> Literally "neither head nor feet."

ne cede malis sed contra audentior ito

nay KAY-deh MAH-lees sehd KAWN-traah ow-DEHN-tih-yawr EE-toh

stand tall

> Virgil counseling us to face up to adversity, literally "do not yield to misfortunes, but go more boldly to meet them."

necesse est ut multos timeat quem multi timent

neh-KEHS-seh ehst uut MUUL-tohs TIH-meh-yaht kwehm MUUL-tee TIH-mehnt

he whom many fear must fear many

> Advice for tyrants from Publilius Syrus.

necessitas dat legem, non ipsa accipit

neh-KEHS-sih-taahs daht LAY-gehm nohn IHP-sah AHK-kih-piht

necessity recognizes no law

> Publilius Syrus telling us literally "necessity gives the law, but does not herself accept it." (For another version of the same thought, see also NECESSITAS NON HABET LEGEM.)

necessitas non habet legem

neh-KEHS-sih-taahs nohn HAH-beht LAY-gehm

necessity has no law

> Watch out. When times are tough enough, many people will stop at nothing to keep their heads above water. (See also VENIA NECESSITATI DATUR.)

necessitas rationum inventrix

neh-KEHS-sih-taahs rah-tih-YOH-nuum ihn-WEHN-
treeks

necessity is the mother of invention

More literally "necessity is the inventor of procedures." Notice that *inventrix* is the feminine form of **inventor** (ihn-WEHN-
tawr), so the English phrase "mother of invention" is especially
appropriate. (See also INGENS TELUM NECESSITAS.)

nec habeo, nec careo, nec curo

nehk HAH-beh-yoh nehk KAAH-reh-yoh nehk KOO-roh

I have not, I want not, I care not

Healthy adjustment to a lack of worldly goods.

nec mora nec requies

nehk MAW-rah nehk REH-kwih-yays

without taking a break

Virgil's phrase, literally "neither delay nor rest."

nec prece nec pretio

nehk PREH-keh nehk PREH-tih-yoh

neither by entreaty nor by bribe

See also VEL PRECE VEL PRETIO.

nec quaerere nec spernere honorem

nehk KWĪ-reh-reh nehk SPEHR-neh-reh haw-NOH-rehm

neither to seek nor to spurn honor

A suitable motto for any truly modest person.

ne credes laudatoribus tuis

nay KRAY-days low-daah-TOH-rih-buus TUU-wees

don't believe those who praise you

> Don't be seduced by flattery.

nec scire fas est omnia

nehk SKEE-reh faahs ehst AWM-nih-yah

don't be a know-it-all

> Horace explaining that much knowledge is inevitably beyond human ken, literally "nor is it possible to know everything."

nec tecum possum vivere nec sine te

nehk TAY-kuum PAWS-suum WEE-weh-reh nehk SIH-neh tay

the forlorn cry of many who love

> Martial putting into words a common plight, literally "I can neither live with you nor without you."

nec temere nec timide

nehk TEH-meh-ray nehk TIH-mih-day

neither rashly nor timidly

nec vixit male qui natus moriensque fefellit

nehk WEEKS-iht MAH-lay kwee NAAH-tuus maw-rih-YAYNS-kweh feh-FEHL-liht

fame isn't everything

> Horace telling us nearly literally "he has not lived ill who has been born and died unnoticed."

ne facias per alium quod fieri potest per te
nay FAH-kih-yaahs pehr AH-lih-yuum kwawd FIH-yeh-ree
PAW-tehst pehr tay

be self-reliant

Literally "do not do through another what you can do all by
yourself."

ne fronti crede
nay FRAWN-tee KRAY-deh

don't judge a book by its cover

Literally "trust not in appearances." (See also BENE NATI, BENE
VESTITI, ET MEDIOCRITER DOCTI.)

ne Iuppiter (or Juppiter) quidem omnibus placet
nay YUUP-pih-tehr KWIH-dehm AWM-nih-buus PLAH-
keht

not even Jupiter can please everyone

So do your best and don't worry.

nemo alius
NAY-moh AH-lih-yuus

no one else

nemo bis punitur pro eodem delicto
NAY-moh bihs POO-nih-tuur proh eh-YOH-dehm day-
LEEK-toh

no double jeopardy

A legal principle, literally "no one is punished twice for the
same offense."

nemo dat quod non habet
NAY-moh daht kwawd nohn HAH-beht

you can't get blood from a stone

Fund-raisers, pay heed to this advice, literally "no one can give what he or she does not have."

nemo in amore videt
NAY-moh ihn ah-MOH-reh WIH-deht
love is blind

Literally "nobody in love sees."

nemo mortalium omnibus horis sapit
NAY-moh mawr-TAAH-lih-yuum AWM-nih-buus HOH-rees SAH-piht
no one bats 1.000

Pliny the Elder telling us "no mortal is always wise." The phrase *omnibus horis*, here given as "always," translates literally as "at all hours."

nemo scit praeter me ubi soccus me pressat
NAY-moh skiht PRĪ-tehr may UU-bee SAWK-kuus may PREHS-saht
don't tell me what's bothering me

Literally "no one except me knows where my shoe hurts." To keep the record straight, *soccus* translates literally as "slipper," most particularly the sock worn by actors in Roman comedies.

nemo solus satis sapit
NAY-moh SOH-luus SAH-tihs SAH-piht
two heads are better than one

Plautus telling us literally "no one is wise enough alone."

ne nimium
nay NIH-mih-yuum
do nothing to excess

Literally "not too much."

ne prius antidotum quam venenum
nay PRIH-yuus ahn-TIH-daw-tuum kwahm weh-NAY-nuum

if it ain't broke, don't fix it

Literally "not the antidote before the poison." (See also QUI-ETA NON MOVERE.)

ne puero gladium
nay PUU-weh-roh GLAH-dih-yuum

don't give a man's job to a boy

Literally "(trust) not a sword to a boy."

nervi belli, pecunia infinita
NEHR-wee BEHL-lee peh-KOO-nih-yah ihn-fee-NEE-tah

when the money dries up, the game is over

Cicero telling us literally "unlimited money is the sinews of war." As well as of most other human undertakings. (See also VECTIGALIA NERVI SUNT REI PUBLICAE.)

nervus probandi
NEHR-wuus praw-BAHN-dee

the chief argument

Literally "the sinew of proof."

nescis quid serus vesper ferat
NEHS-kees kwihd SAY-ruus WEHS-pehr FEH-raht

you don't know what the night may bring

nescit plebs ieiuna (or jejuna) timere
NAYS-kiht playbs yay-YOO-nah tih-MAY-reh

ripe for revolution

Lucan observing that "a hungry populace does not know how to fear."

nescit vox missa reverti
NAYS-kiht vohks MEE-sah reh-WEHR-tee
think twice before sounding off

Horace telling us that "a word once uttered cannot be turned back."

nihil ad rem
NIH-hihl ahd rehm
irrelevant

Literally "nothing to do with the matter."

nihil amori iniuriam (or injuriam) est
NIH-hihl ah-MOH-ree ihn-YOO-rih-yahm ehst
there is nothing that love will not forgive

Except forgetting to dry the dishes and take out the garbage.

nil conscire sibi, nulla pallescere culpa
neel kohn-SKEE-reh SIH-bih NOOL-laah pahl-LAYS-keh-reh KUUL-paah
to be able to sleep at night

Horace telling us how good it feels literally "to feel no guilt, to pale at no blame."

nil debet
neel DAY-beht
he owes nothing

nil dictum quod non dictum prius
neel DIHK-tuum kwawd nohn DIHK-tuum PRIH-yuus
how hard it is to be original

> Literally "nothing has been said that has not been said before."

nil magnum nisi bonum
neel MAHG-nuum NIH-sih BAW-nuum
nothing is great unless (it's) good

> Not evil, that is.

nil mortalibus arduum est
neel mawr-TAAH-lih-buus AHR-duu-wuum ehst
nothing is (too) difficult for human beings

nil sine magno vita labore dedit mortalibus
neel SIH-neh MAHG-noh WEE-tah lah-BOH-reh DEH-
diht mawr-TAAH-lih-buus
no pain, no gain

> Horace telling us literally that "life has given nothing to man-
kind without great labor."

nitimur in vetitum semper, cupimusque negata
NEE-tih-muur ihn WEH-tih-tuum SEHM-pehr kuu-pih-
MUUS-kweh neh-GAAH-tah
forbidden fruits are sweetest

> Ovid telling us literally "we are always striving for what is
forbidden, and desiring what is denied us."

nitor in adversum
NEE-tawr ihn ahd-WEHR-suum
I struggle against misfortune

> A phrase from a resolute Ovid.

nobilitas sola est atque unice virtus
noh-BIH-lih-taahs SOH-lah ehst AHT-kweh OO-nih-kay
WIHR-toos

virtue is the one and only nobility

According to Juvenal. (See also STEMMATA QUID FACIUNT?)

nobis iudicibus (or judicibus)
NOH-bees yoo-DIH-kih-buus

in our opinion

Literally "we being judges."

nocet empta dolore voluptas
NAW-keht AYMP-tah daw-LOH-reh waw-LUUP-taahs

let's keep things within bounds

Horace telling us literally that "pleasure gained from pain is
harmful." Could the Marquis de Sade have had it wrong?

noli irritare leones
NOH-lee ihr-ree-TAAH-reh leh-YOH-nays

do not provoke the lions

Don't look for trouble. (See also ADVERSA VIRTUTE REPELLO.)

nolo episcopari
NOH-loh eh-pees-kaw-PAAH-ree

I do not choose to run

An elegant Latin phrase, translated literally as "I do not wish
to be a bishop," to use when turning down an appointment or
nomination for high office.

nomina stultorum parietibus haerent
NOH-mih-nah stuul-TOH-ruum pah-rih-YEH-tih-buus HĪ-rehnt

fools' names stick to the walls (of buildings)

This saying is usually given in English as a jingle, writer unknown:

> Fools' names, like fools' faces,
> Are always found in public places.

Whether given in Latin or in English, this thought is certainly not intended as a compliment. Graffiti artists were known even in ancient Pompeii, where visitors can still see their wall scribblings.

nominis umbra
NOH-mih-nihs UUM-brah

the shadow of a name

Lucan gave us this phrase, useful for describing a person or family of bygone eminence. It appears in his observation **stat magni** (staht MAHG-nee) **nominis umbra**, "there remains the shadow of a great name."

non culpabilis
nohn kuul-PAAH-bih-lihs

not guilty

A verdict exonerating a person on trial.

non datur tertium
nohn DAH-tuur TEHR-tih-yuum

yes or no, nothing in between

The phrase to use, literally "no third (choice) is given," when adjuring someone to choose one or the other of two paths, two actions, two candidates, or the like.

non decet
nohn DEH-keht
it is not proper

non deficiente crumena
nohn day-fih-kih-YEHN-teh kruu-MAY-naah
as long as the money holds out

A phrase from Horace, literally "the purse not failing," who recognized that money counts for much. (See also ET GENUS ET FORMAM REGINA PECUNIA DONAT.)

non est fumus absque igne
nohn ehst FOO-muus AHBS-kweh IHG-neh
there is no smoke without fire

This proverb, in English dating back to the fifteenth century, tells us that every rumor or slander has some basis in fact. Maybe.

non est iocus (or jocus) esse malignum
nohn ehst YAW-kuus EHS-seh mah-LEEG-nuum
jokes that hurt aren't funny

Horace telling us literally "there is no fun where there is spite."

non ex quovis ligno Mercurius fit
nohn ehks KWOH-wees LIHG-noh mehr-KUU-rih-yuus fiht
you can't make a silk purse out of a sow's ear

We have long been told that you cannot make something good out of something that is by nature inferior in quality, here expressed literally in Latin as "you cannot make a (statue of) Mercury out of just any log." Mercury, known primarily by modern people as the messenger of the Roman gods, was also the god of eloquence, skill, trading, and thieving. Overlooking for now Mercury's last area of responsibility, we can take it that Mercury was someone worthy of high regard. Thus, the use of any ordinary wood for a statue of Mercury would surely be seen as demeaning.

non generant aquilae columbas
nohn GEH-neh-rahnt AH-kwih-lī kaw-LUUM-baahs
eagles do not bear doves

non ministrari, sed ministrare
nohn mih-nihs-TRAAH-ree sehd mih-nihs-TRAAH-reh
not to be ministered to, but to minister

Motto of Wellesley College.

non multa sed multum
nohn MUUL-tah sehd MUUL-tuum
what is desired is quality, not quantity

Literally "not many things, but much." (See also PAUCA SED BONA.)

non nobis solum nati sumus
nohn NOH-bees SOH-luum NAAH-tee SUU-muus
not for ourselves alone are we born

non omne licitum honestum
nohn AWM-neh LIH-kih-tuum haw-NEHS-tuum
not every lawful thing is honorable

Perhaps this saying ought to be made part of the oath taken by newly installed public servants. It is not enough merely to observe the letter of the law.

non possidentem multa vocaveris recte beatum

nohn paws-sih-DEHN-tehm MUUL-tah waw-KAAH-weh-rihs RAYK-tay beh-YAAH-tuum

money isn't everything

Horace telling us literally "you cannot rightly call happy the man who possesses many things."

non progredi est regredi

nohn proh-GREH-dee ehst reh-GREH-dee

not to go forward is to go backward

A good motto for self-styled progressives.

non quis sed quid

nohn kwihs sehd kwihd

not who but what

The message is clear: Don't ask who says it, examine what is being said.

non revertar inultus

nohn reh-WEHR-tahr ihn-UUL-tuus

I shall not return unavenged

A bold and resolute assertion by an ancient military commander who meant he would not return home without having avenged a prior defeat. In modern history, World War II general Douglas MacArthur asserted to his Filipino allies, "I shall return." Implicit in this statement was a vow to fight on to victory, and thus avenge his ignominious earlier defeat in defending the Philippine Islands.

non scribit cuius carmina nemo legit

nohn SKREE-biht KOOWEE-yuus KAHR-mih-nah NAY-moh LEH-giht

when a tree falls unheard in a forest

Martial passing a sad judgment on readers if not on writers, literally "he (or she) is no writer whose verses no one reads." Maybe just a bad writer.

non sibi sed patriae
nohn SIH-bih sehd PAH-trih-yī
not for self but for country

nostro periculo
NAWS-troh peh-REE-kuu-loh
at our own risk

> See also MEO PERICULO.

notabilia
naw-taah-BIH-lih-yah
things worthy of note

> See also NOTATU DIGNUM.

notandum
noh-TAHN-duum
a memorandum

> Literally "something to be noted."

notatu dignum
noh-TAAH-too DIHG-nuum
worthy of note

> See also NOTABILIA.

novus rex, nova lex
NAW-wuus rayks NAW-wah layks
it's a new ball game every time

Literally "new king, new law." This adage had greater currency in past times, when wars of conquest seemed to be a popular sport and nations frequently found themselves falling under foreign rule. Each time a new ruler took over the reins of government, he called the shots. Of course, the sport is by no means archaic.

noxiae poena par esto
NAWKS-ih-yī POY-nah paahr EHS-toh
let the punishment match the offense

Cicero proposing that punishment for a crime be made appropriate to the severity of the crime. (See also CULPAE POENA PAR ESTO.)

nuda veritas
NOO-dah WAY-rih-taahs
naked truth

Horace gave us this phrase, also translated as "undisguised truth *or* unvarnished truth."

nudis oculis
NOO-dees AW-kuu-lees
with the naked eyes

Without a telescope, microscope, or the like, that is.

nudis verbis
NOO-dees WEHR-bees
in plain words

nugae canorae
NOO-gī kah-NOH-rī
melodious trifles

A condemnation.

nugae litterariae
NOO-gī liht-teh-RAAH-rih-yī
literary trifles

A condemnation.

nugis addere pondus
NOO-gees AHD-deh-reh PAWN-duus
to try to make something out of nothing

A phrase from Horace, literally "to add weight to trifles."

nulla regula sine exceptione
NOOL-lah RAY-guu-lah SIH-neh ehks-kehp-tih-YOH-neh
no rule without an exception

nulli desperandum quamdiu spirat
NOOL-lee day-spay-RAHN-duum KWAHM-dih-yoo
SPEE-raht
while there's life there's hope

Literally "no one is to be despaired of so long as he breathes."
Without an artificial respirator? Also expressed as **dum spiro
spero** (duum SPEE-roh SPAY-roh), "while I breathe, I hope," a
motto of South Carolina.

nulli sapere casu obtigit
NOOL-lee SAH-peh-reh KAAH-soo AWB-tih-giht
people are struck dumb but never struck wise

Seneca the Younger telling us literally that "no one ever became wise by chance." It takes many years and the right natural
endowment to become wise.

nullius addictus iurare (or jurare) in verba magistri

nool-LEE-yuus ahd-DIHK-tuus yoo-RAAH-reh ihn
WEHR-bah mah-GIHS-tree

his own man

Horace characterizing his own sense of independence, literally "not bound to swear to the words of any master."

nunc vino pellite curas

nuunk WEE-noh PEHL-lih-teh KOO-raahs

now banish cares with wine

Horace offering advice for those who are heavily burdened. (See also ERGO BIBAMUS!)

nunquam dormio

NUUN-kwahm DAWR-mih-yoh

I am ever vigilant

Literally "I never sleep."

O

obscuris vera involvens

awb-SKOO-rees WAY-rah ihn-WAWL-wayns

shrouding truth in obscurity

Virgil's phrase defining the uncommon word "obfuscation," a common technique practiced by uncommonly clever people intent on confusing voters, listeners, or readers. (See also VERITAS NIHIL VERETUR NISI ABSCONDI.)

obsequium amicos, veritas odium parit

awb-SEH-kwih-yuum ah-MEE-kohs WAY-rih-taahs
AW-dih-yuum PAH-riht

compliance breeds friends, truth hatred

ob turpem causam
awb TUUR-pehm KOW-sahm
for a base cause

ob vitae solatium
awb WEE-tī soh-LAH-tih-yuum
for comfort or pleasure

> Literally "for the solace of life."

occasio furem facit
awk-KAAH-sih-yoh FOO-rehm FAH-kiht
don't forget to lock your car

> Literally "opportunity makes the thief."

odi memorem compotorem
OH-dee MEH-maw-rehm kawm-poh-TOH-rehm
I hate a drinking friend with a memory

> Recognition that we are apt to speak imprudently while under the influence.

odor lucri
AW-dawr LUU-kree
expectation of gain

> Literally "the smell of wealth." (See also LUCRI BONUS EST ODOR.)

O fortunatos nimium, sua si bona norint!
oh fohr-too-NAAH-tohs NIH-mih-yuum SUU-wah see BAW-nah NOH-rihnt
count your blessings

> Virgil had farmers in mind when he said, "O too happy they, if they but knew their blessings!" but he gave many of the rest of us something to think about.

O imitatores, servum pecus!
oh ih-mih-tah-TOH-rays SEHR-wuum PEH-kuus
O imitators, you slavish herd!

Horace's phrase, especially useful in discussions of a literary or artistic nature. (See also IMITATORES, SERVUM PECUS.)

ollae amicitia
AWL-lī ah-mee-KIH-tih-yah
cupboard love

Literally translated as "friendship of the pot." Cupboard love is affection insincerely professed or displayed to obtain a favor. Narrowly defined, cupboard love is cozying up to a cook in the expectation of obtaining special or generous servings of food.

olla male fervet
AWL-lah MAH-lay FEHR-weht
the affair is going badly

Another culinary metaphor, literally "the pot boils badly," used to characterize disintegrating affairs of daily life, whether commercial or amorous. (See OLLAE AMICITIA.)

omen faustum
OH-mehn FOWS-tuum
an auspicious omen *or* an inauspicious sign

O mihi praeteritos referat si Iuppiter (or **Juppiter**) annos
oh MIH-hih prī-TEH-rih-tohs REH-feh-raht see YUUP-pih-tehr AHN-nohs
would that I were young again

A wistful Virgil looking back with regret: "O that Jupiter would give me back the years that are past."

omne solum forti patria est

AWM-neh SAW-luum FAWR-tee PAH-trih-yah ehst

to the brave every land is a homeland

A brave person is willing to go anywhere, even to a strange land.

omne vitium in proclivi est

AWM-neh WIH-tih-yuum ihn proh-KLEE-wee ehst

one misstep leads to another

This caution tells us literally that "every vice is downhill." Also expressed as **facilis descensus Averno** (FAH-kih-lihs days-KAYN-suus ah-WEHR-noh), "the descent to hell is easy." **Avernus** (ah-WEHR-nuus) was the entrance to the lower world, or the lower world itself. (See also HAEC NUGAE IN SERIA DUCENT MALA and PRINCIPIIS OBSTA.)

omnia bona bonis

AWM-nih-yah BAW-nah BAW-nees

be good but don't be naive

This observation, literally "to the good, all things are good," decries credulity.

omnia mea mecum porto

AWM-nih-yah MEH-yah MAY-kuum PAWR-toh

I scorn earthly goods

Literally "I carry with me everything that is mine." The intent here is not to glorify the backpack, but to plug frugality.

omnia mors aequat

AWM-nih-yah mawrs Ī-kwaht

the great equalizer

Claudian telling us literally that "death levels all things."

omnia praeclara rara
AWM-nih-yah prī-KLAAH-rah RAAH-rah
all splendid things are rare

Cicero telling us not to expect to find in life too much that is truly outstanding.

omnia suspendens naso
AWM-nih-yah suus-PEHN-dayns NAH-soh
turning up one's nose at everything

See also SUSPENDENS OMNIA NASO.

omnibus has litteras visuris
AWM-nih-buus haahs LIHT-teh-raahs wee-SOO-rees
to whom it may concern

Literally "to all who see this document."

omnibus invideas, livide, nemo tibi
AWM-nih-buus ihn-WIH-deh-yaahs LEE-wih-deh NAY-moh TIH-bih
envy is not an endearing attribute

Literally "you may envy everybody, envious one, but nobody envies you." (See also QUI INVIDET MINOR EST.)

omnis amans amens
AWM-nihs AH-maahns AAH-mayns
every lover is out of his (or her) mind

Also given as **amantes sunt amentes** (ah-MAHN-tays suunt aah-MEHN-tays), "lovers are lunatics."

operae pretium est
AW-peh-rī PREH-tih-yuum ehst
it is worthwhile

Terence telling us literally "there is reward for the work"; that is, the work is worth doing.

operose nihil agunt
aw-peh-ROH-say NIH-hihl AH-guunt
they are doing nothing busily

Seneca the Younger's observation of time wasters, who are trying not to work and are fooling no one but themselves. (See also OTIOSA SEDULITAS.)

opposuit natura
awp-PAW-suu-wiht naah-TOO-rah
it is unnatural

Also rendered as "it is contrary to nature," or literally as "nature has opposed."

optima interpres legum consuetudo

See CONSUETUDO EST OPTIMA INTERPRES LEGUM.

optimi consiliarii mortui
AWP-tih-mee kohn-sih-lih-AAH-rih-yee MAWR-too-wee
learn from the past

Literally "the best counselors are the dead." We ignore ancient wisdom at our own peril.

optimum obsonium labor
AWP-tih-muum awb-SOH-nih-yuum LAH-bawr
work is the best appetizer

More literally "work is the best means of getting a meal." And the New Testament tells us, "If any would not work, neither should he eat." Of special interest in the Latin phrase is the word *obsonium*, which is defined as "food, usually fish, eaten with bread." Thus, it can be thought of as an hors d'oeuvre, from the

French, literally "outside the work." What goes around, comes around.

opum furiata cupido
AW-puum fuu-rih-YAAH-tah kuu-PEE-doh
a frenzied lust for wealth

> Ovid's phrase for the motivation that drives too many of us.

opus opificem probat
AW-puus aw-PIH-fih-kehm PRAW-baht
the work proves the craftsperson

> This maxim need not be applied exclusively to the traditional crafts. It's what we accomplish in any field that counts, not the glorified appellation we claim for our profession.

orate, fratres
oh-RAAH-teh FRAH-trays
pray, brothers

ore rotundo
OH-reh raw-TUUN-doh
with well-turned speech

> Horace describing the smooth delivery of a fine orator, literally "with a round mouth."

ossa atque pellis totus est
AWS-sah AHT-kweh PEHL-lihs TOH-tuus ehst
he is all skin and bones

> Plautus giving us what has become and remained a vivid English cliché for the noun "emaciation." To describe a woman, change to **ossa atque pellis tota** (TOH-tah) **ehst**.

O ter quaterque beati!
oh tehr kwah-TEHR-kweh beh-YAAH-tee
O thrice and four times blessed are they!

A happy phrase from Virgil.

otia dant vitia
OH-tih-yah dahnt WIH-tih-yah
the devil finds work for idle hands

Literally "leisure begets vices."

otiosa sedulitas
oh-tih-YOH-sah say-DUU-lih-taahs
idle assiduity

This oxymoron suggests that some of us are capable of laborious trifling—busy work. Not true of most of us. (See also OPEROSE NIHIL AGUNT and STRENUA INERTIA.)

otium sine dignitate
OH-tih-yuum SIH-neh dihg-nih-TAAH-teh
leisure without dignity

The opposite of **otium cum** (kuum) **dignitate,** "leisure with dignity."

otium sine litteris mors est
OH-tih-yuum SIH-neh LIHT-teh-rees mawrs ehst
take books along next summer

Seneca the Younger telling us "leisure without literature is death." The phrase *sine litteris* can also be translated as "uncultured," but we would not say "uncultured leisure."

P

pabulum animi
PAAH-buu-luum AH-nih-mee
learning

> Literally "food for the mind."

pacta conventa
PAHK-tah kawn-WEHN-tah
a diplomatic pact

> Literally "the conditions agreed upon."

pactum illicitum
PAHK-tuum ihl-LIH-kih-tuum
an unlawful agreement

pallidus ira
PAHL-lih-duus EE-raah
pale with rage

palmam qui meruit ferat
PAHL-mahm kwee MEH-ruu-wiht FEH-raht
may the best man win

> The motto, literally "let him bear the palm who has deserved it," of Lord Nelson (1758–1805), the great British admiral. In ancient Rome, a victorious gladiator was given a branch of the palm tree. Thus "bear the palm" means "be the best."

palma non sine pulvere
PAHL-mah nohn SIH-neh PUUL-weh-reh

no gain without pain

A Roman proverb, literally "the palm not without effort," telling us that no one achieves success without struggle. For another meaning of **pulvis** (PUUL-wihs), the nominative form of the ablative *pulvere,* see PULVIS ET UMBRA SUMUS. (See also PALMAM QUI MERUIT FERAT for the significance of "palm.")

par bene comparatum
paahr BEH-neh kawm-pah-RAAH-tuum

a well-matched pair

parce, parce, precor
PAHR-keh PAHR-keh PREH-kawr

spare me, spare me, I pray

parcere subiectis (or subjectis) et debellare superbos
PAHR-keh-reh suub-YEHK-tees eht day-behl-LAAH-reh suu-PEHR-bohs

to spare the vanquished and subdue the proud

Virgil explaining the balanced aim of Roman conquest.

parem non feret
PAAH-rehm nohn FEH-reht

he (or she) brooks no equal

The mind-set of the egocentric person.

paritur pax bello
PAH-rih-tuur paahks BEHL-loh

peace is born of war

See also ARMA TUENTUR PACEM.

par negotiis neque supra
paahr neh-GOH-tih-yees NEH-kweh SUU-praah
vocational bliss

Literally "equal to work and not above it." Tacitus describing a person well suited to his or her occupation.

par oneri
pahr AW-neh-ree
equal to the burden

pars pro toto
pahrs proh TOH-toh
synecdoche

Literally "a part for the whole." Saying "we need new faces" rather than "we need new employees" is an example of synecdoche—the rhetorical use of a part to represent the whole.

pars sanitatis velle sanari fuit
pahrs saah-nih-TAAH-tihs WEHL-leh saah-NAAH-ree FUU-wiht
to be cured one must wish to be cured

An insight from Seneca the Younger remarkable for its time, literally "part of health is to want to be healed."

parva componere magnis
PAHR-wah kawm-POH-neh-reh MAHG-nees
to compare small things with great

parvis componere magna
PAHR-wees kawm-POH-neh-reh MAHG-nah
to compare great things with small

parvis e glandibus quercus
PAHR-wees ay GLAHN-dih-buus KWEHR-kuus
the mighty oak from little acorns grows

Great things have small beginnings. (See also GUTTA CAVAT LAPIDEM, CONSUMITUR ANULUS USU.)

parvum parva decent
PAHR-wuum PAHR-wah DEH-kehnt
small things befit the humble person

An adage from Horace implying that great things befit the proud or ambitious person.

patres conscripti
PAH-trays kohn-SKREEP-tee
legislators

Literally "the conscript fathers," by definition the patrician and the elected plebeian members of the ancient Roman Senate. The phrase derives from the enrollment of senators by Junius Brutus (85–42 B.C.), the first Roman consul.

patria cara, carior libertas
PAH-trih-yah KAAH-rah KAAH-rih-yawr lee-BEHR-taahs
my native land is dear, but liberty is dearer

patriae infelici fidelis
PAH-trih-yī een-fay-LEE-kee fih-DAY-lihs
faithful to my unhappy country

patria potestas
PAH-trih-yah paw-TEHS-taahs
parental authority

A legal term for the power of a Roman father over his family, a power not inconsiderable when compared with the role of the modern father in most parts of the world. At one time a Roman father even had power of life and limb over his wife and children.

pauca sed bona
POW-kah sehd BAW-nah
not quantity but quality

A motto, literally "a few things but good," often given as "less is more." (See also NON MULTA SED MULTUM.)

paucis verbis
POW-kees WEHR-bees
in few words

paulo maiora (or majora) canamus
POW-loh mah-YOH-rah kah-NAAH-muus
let us sing of somewhat loftier things

From Virgil, who sang of loftier things.

paulum morati, serius aut citius sedem properamus ad unam
POW-luum maw-RAAH-tee SAY-rih-yuus owt KIH-tih-yuus SAY-dehm praw-peh-RAAH-muus ahd OO-nahm
we all must die one day

Ovid on the inevitability of death, literally "after a slight delay, sooner or later we hasten to one and the same abode." (See what Horace had to say on this subject in PULVIS ET UMBRA SUMUS.)

pectus est quod disertos facit
PEHK-tuus ehst kwawd dih-SEHR-tohs FAH-kiht
speak from the heart

Quintilian telling us how to become successful orators, literally "it is the heart that makes persons eloquent." So when you speak from the heart, the words will take care of themselves. We hope. (See also REM TENE ET VERBA SEQUENTUR.)

pedibus timor addidit alas
PEH-dih-buus TIH-mawr AHD-dih-diht AAH-laahs
a good scare can turn you into an Olympic sprinter

An adage from Virgil, literally "fear has added wings to one's feet."

Pelio imponere Ossam
PAY-lih-yoh ihm-POH-neh-reh AWS-sahm
to pile hardship upon hardship

Literally "to pile Ossa upon Pelion," but also freely rendered in English as "to pile embarrassment upon embarrassment." Pelion and Ossa are both mountain peaks in Thessaly. In the *Odyssey*, when the giants wanted to climb to heaven and destroy the gods, they piled Ossa and Pelion together to reach Olympus, the lofty home of the gods. Pelion was the home of the centaurs.

per aetatem
pehr ī-TAAH-tehm
by reason of one's age

per aevum
pehr Ī-wuum
forever

Literally "for eternity."

per ambages
pehr ahm-BAAH-gays
beating around the bush

This phrase can be rendered literally as "by windings," more felicitously as "by circumlocution" or "by quibbling."

per aspera ad astra
pehr AHS-peh-rah ahd AHS-trah

through difficulties to the stars

Also given as **ad astra per aspera**, the motto of Kansas. Either way, this well-known saying has nothing to do with the Hubble Space Telescope, but teaches that we achieve great things only by encountering and overcoming adversity.

percontatorem fugito, nam garrulus idem est
pehr-kawn-taah-TOH-rehm FUU-gih-toh nahm GAHR-ruu-luus EE-dehm ehst

watch out for snoopers

Horace providing a worthwhile proverb, literally "shun an inquisitive man, for he is sure to be a gossip."

pereunt et imputantur
PEH-reh-yuunt eht ihm-puu-TAHN-tuur

how time passes

A sundial inscription, almost literally "they (the hours or years) pass away and are charged to one's account."

per gradus
pehr GRAH-doos

step by step

periculum fortitudine evasi
peh-REE-kuu-luum fawr-tih-TOO-dih-neh ay-WAAH-see

by courage I have escaped danger

Others have succeeded by less audacious means.

per iocum (or jocum)
pehr YAW-kuum
for fun

Also rendered as "in jest" and "by way of a joke."

peritis in sua arte credendum
peh-REE-tees ihn SUU-waah AHR-teh kray-DEHN-duum
watch out for the know-it-all

Literally "the experts should be trusted in their own areas of competence." But not outside them.

per legem terrae
pehr LAY-gehm TEHR-rī
by the law of the land

pernicibus alis
pehr-NEE-kih-buus AAH-lees
rapidly

Virgil's phrase, literally "with swift wings."

per pares
pehr PAAH-rays
by one's peers

perpetuum mobile
pehr-PEH-tuu-wuum MOH-bih-leh
perpetual motion

More accurately rendered as "something perpetually in motion."

per saltum
pehr SAHL-tuum

by a leap

This phrase may also be rendered as "without intermediate stages" or "skipping over intermediate stages."

per tot discrimina rerum
pehr tawt dihs-KREE-mih-nah RAY-ruum

through so many critical moments

Virgil's phrase.

pia desideria
PIH-yah day-see-DEH-rih-yah

pious regrets

pia fraus
PIH-yah frows

a pious fraud

Ovid's phrase. Also given as FRAUS PIA.

piscem natare doces
PIHS-kehm nah-TAAH-reh DAW-kays

you are wasting your time

Literally "you are teaching a fish to swim," also rendered traditionally as "you're carrying coals to Newcastle." (See also IN SILVAM LIGNA FERRE.)

pleno iure (or jure)
PLAY-noh YOO-reh

with full authority

plus in posse quam in actu
ploos ihn PAWS-seh kwahm ihn AAHK-too
more in possibility than in fact

Useful in suggesting that something described as existing may not really exist at all.

plus minusve
ploos mih-NUUS-weh
more or less

populus me sibilat, at mihi plaudo
PAW-puu-luus may SEE-bih-laht aht MIH-hih PLOW-doh
who cares what people say?

Horace, who did not quake when facing rejection, telling us literally "the people hiss me, but I applaud myself." Like the advice given by Shakespeare's Polonius, "This above all—to thine own self be true," a motto for all who have faith in themselves.

posse videor
PAWS-seh WIH-deh-yawr
I seem to be able

A phrase that may be taken as anticipating the mantra "I think I can, I think I can," of *The Little Engine That Could.*

post bellum auxilium
pawst BEHL-luum owks-IH-lih-yuum
where were you when I needed you?

A sad phrase, literally "help after the war," for help that comes too late. Bosnia, Rwanda, Somalia, Sudan . . .

post factum nullum consilium
pawst FAHK-tuum NOOL-lum kohn-SIH-lih-yuum
now you tell me!

> Literally "after the deed, no advice is helpful."

post litem motam
pawst LEE-tehm MOH-tahm
after litigation began

> A phrase in law.

post obitum
pawst AW-bih-tuum
after death

post prandium
pawst PRAHN-dih-yuum
after a meal

post proelia praemia
pawst PROY-lih-yah PRĪ-mih-yah
after battles, rewards

> For the victors, that is.

post tenebras lux
pawst TEH-neh-braahs looks
after darkness, light

> After despair, news bringing hope.

potior est conditio possidentis
PAW-tih-yawr ehst kawn-DIH-tih-yoh paws-sih-DEHN-tihs
possession is nine-tenths of the law

Literally the "the condition of the possessor is preferable."

praemia virtutis
PRĪ-mih-yah wihr-TOO-tihs
the rewards of virtue

praemissis praemittendis
prī-MEES-sees prī-miht-TEHN-dees
getting to the point

Ironically, this succinct phrase requires a rather long-winded translation: "having placed in the preface things that should be placed in the preface" (so that important matters may be addressed at once).

praesto et persto
PRĪ-stoh eht PEHR-stoh
I stand in front and I stand fast

The attitude of the valiant leader, willing to expose himself or herself to attack and never retreat.

praeteriti anni
prī-TEH-rih-tee AHN-nee
bygone years

pretio parata vincitur pretio fides
PREH-tih-yoh pah-RAAH-tah WIHN-kih-tuur PREH-tih-yoh FIH-days
loyalty isn't for sale

This proverb, literally "loyalty gained through bribes is lost through bribes," warns against trying to buy friendship.

prima caritas incipit a se ipso
PREE-mah KAAH-rih-taahs IHN-kih-piht aah say IHP-soh
charity begins at home

> Literally "charity begins first with oneself."

primo intuitu
PREE-moh ihn-TUU-wih-too
at first glance

primo mihi
PREE-moh MIH-hih
for myself first

primum non nocere
PREE-muum nohn naw-KAY-reh
first of all, do no harm

> A medical aphorism adjuring the physician to avoid employ-
> ing a remedy that is worse than the disease to be cured.

principia, non homines
preen-KIH-pih-yah nohn HAW-mih-nays
the rule of law, not the rule of men

> Literally "principles, not men."

principibus placuisse viris non ultima laus est
preen-KIH-pih-buus plah-kuu-WIHS-seh WIH-rees nohn
OOL-tih-mah lows ehst
the best praise is that given by qualified critics

> Horace, who had his share of recognition, telling us literally
> "to have won the approbation of eminent men is not the lowest
> praise."

principiis obsta
preen-KIH-pih-yees AWB-staah
resist the beginnings

It's the first misstep that counts, and the first indiscretion leads inevitably to more. (See also HAEC NUGAE SERIA DUCENT IN MALA and OMNE VITIUM IN PROCLIVI EST.)

prior tempore, prior iure (or jure)
PRIH-yāwr TEHM-paw-reh PRIH-yawr YOO-reh
first come, first served

Literally "first in time, first by right."

pristinae virtutis memores
prees-TEE-nī wihr-TOO-tihs MEH-maw-rays
mindful of the valor of former days

Everything was better in the old days.

probitas verus honor
PRAW-bih-taahs WAY-ruus HAW-nawr
honesty is true honor

Because it takes courage to be completely honest.

prodesse quam conspici
proh-DEHS-seh kwahm KOHN-spih-kee
to be of service rather than to be gazed at

The reason why the best of us do our best.

pro et contra
proh eht KAWN-traah
for and against

pro forma tantum
proh FAWR-maah TAHN-tuum
for form only

> Just for appearances.

pro libertate patriae
proh lee-behr-TAAH-teh PAH-trih-yī
for the liberty of my country

pro nunc
proh nuunk
for now

proprio iure (or **jure**)
PRAW-prih-yoh YOO-reh
in one's own right

proprio vigore
PRAW-prih-yoh wih-GOH-reh
independently

> Literally "of one's own strength" or "by its own force."

pro pudor!
proh PUU-dawr
for shame!

pro virili parte
proh wih-REE-lee PAHR-teh
to the best of one's ability

> All one can ask of anyone.

pro virtute felix temeritas
proh wihr-TOO-teh FAY-leeks teh-MEH-rih-taahs
in place of courage a lucky foolhardiness

Beats cowardice.

pugnis et calcibus
PUUG-nees eht KAHL-kih-buus
tooth and nail

To win in an important struggle, you are well advised to go at it with all you have, literally "with fists and heels."

pulvis et umbra sumus
PUUL-wihs eht UUM-brah SUU-muus
in the end we are nothing

Horace, in a poignant reminder of our mortality, telling us literally "we are but dust and shadow." (For Ovid on death, see PAULUM MORATI, SERIUS AUT CITIUS SEDEM PROPERAMUS AD UNAM.)

Q

quae amissa salva
kwī aah-MEES-sah SAHL-wah
things lost are safe

Perhaps in the sense that they cannot be lost a second time.

quae e longinquo magis placent
kwī ay lawn-GEEN-kwoh MAH-gihs PLAH-kehnt
distance lends enchantment

Literally "things from afar please the more." Two other phrases are often seen that convey the same meaning: **maior** (or **major**) **e longinquo reverentia** (MAH-yawr ay lawn-GEEN-kwoh reh-weh-REHN-tih-yah), "greater reverence from afar," and **omne ignotum pro magnifico est** (AWM-neh ihg-NOH-tuum proh mahg-NIH-fih-koh ehst), "everything unknown is thought magnificent."

quae fuerunt vitia mores sunt
kwī fuu-WAY-ruunt WIH-tih-yah MOH-rays suunt
what once were vices now are customs

Seneca the Younger commenting on what he perceived as a decline in public values. Cole Porter observed the same decline, but with characteristic jocularity gave us "now, goodness knows, anything goes."

quae non valeant singula iuncta (or juncta) iuvant (or juvant)
kwī nohn WAH-leh-yahnt SIHN-guu-lah YOONK-tah YUU-wahnt
united we stand, divided we fall

Literally "things that do not avail singly are effective when united."

quaestio vexata
KWĪS-tih-yoh wayks-AAH-tah
a vexing *or* distressing question

A question that touches on sensitive matters or a disputed question. Also given as VEXATA QUAESTIO.

qualis rex, talis grex
KWAAH-lihs rayks TAAH-lihs grehks
as the shepherd, so the flock

The Latin phrase speaks of a king (*rex*) and a flock (*grex*), making some editors unhappy because of what they perceive as a mixed metaphor, but the phrase in its entirety is in common use to convey the meaning that the nature of a people is largely determined by the nature of its leadership. And we are left with the inference that *qualis rex, talis grex,* literally "as the king, so the flock," can be applied to other types of organizations, including sports teams, businesses, and schools.

qualis vir, talis oratio

KWAAH-lihs wihr TAAH-lihs oh-RAAH-tih-yoh

as the man, so the speech

So maybe words do not always make the man (or the woman). Here we are told that the opposite claim can also be valid.

qualis vita, finis ita

KWAAH-lihs WEE-tah FEE-nihs IH-tah

as the life, so the death

The word *finis* can, of course, also be translated as "end," with the thought remaining the same—a good life ends in a good way, a bad life in an end less satisfactory.

quamdiu se bene gesserit

KWAHM-dih-yoo say BEH-neh GEHS-seh-riht

during good behavior

Parolees and students should keep this phrase in mind as a requirement for continuing privileges. Its literal translation is "as long as he (or she) behaves well."

quam parva sapientia mundus regitur!

kwahm PAHR-waah sah-pih-YEHN-tih-yaah MUUN-duus REH-gih-tuur

with how little wisdom the world is governed!

And things are not getting any better—or are they?

quam primum
kwahm PREE-muum

as soon as possible

If not immediately or forthwith, both of which adverbs can be used as translations of *quam primum*.

quam proxime
kwahm PRAWKS-ih-may

as nearly as possible

quanti est sapere!
KWAHN-tee ehst SAH-peh-reh

how grand it is to be wise!

A phrase from Terence that can be used literally or sardonically.

quantum mutatus ab illo!
KWAHN-tuum moo-TAAH-tuus ahb IHL-loh

how much changed from the man he was!

Virgil giving us the phrase of choice for gossiping about a person who has become altered in appearance or character.

quasi dictum
KWAH-sih DIHK-tuum

as if said

quasi dixisset
KWAH-sih deeks-IHS-seht

as if he (or she) had said

quem Iuppiter (or Juppiter) vult perdere, prius dementat

kwehm YUUP-pih-tehr wuult PEHR-deh-reh PRIH-yuus day-MEHN-taht

whom Jupiter wishes to destroy, he first makes mad

So that he will destroy himself.

qui capit ille facit

kwee KAH-piht IHL-leh FAH-kiht

if the shoe fits, wear it

Literally "he who takes it (a disparaging remark) on himself has done it."

quicquid praecipies esto brevis

KWIHK-kwihd prī-KIH-pih-yays EH-stoh BREH-wihs

keep it short

Horace giving us a valid lesson in rhetoric, literally "whatever you're trying to teach us, be brief."

qui dedit beneficium taceat; narret qui accepit

kwee DEH-diht beh-neh-FIH-kih-yuum TAH-keh-yaht NAHR-reht kwee ahk-KAY-piht

don't boast about your acts of charity

Seneca the Younger telling us not to embarrass a person we help, literally "let the person who performed the kind act keep silent; let the recipient tell about it."

quid hoc sibi vult?

kwihd hohk SIH-bih wuult

what does this mean?

quid leges sine moribus vanae proficiunt?
kwihd LAY-gays SIH-neh MOH-rih-buus WAAH-nī proh-FIH-kih-yuunt

you can't legislate morality

Literally "of what use are idle laws in the absence of morals?"

quid non mortalia pectora cogis, auri sacra fames?
kwihd nohn mawr-TAAH-lih-yah PEHK-taw-rah KOH-gihs OW-ree SAH-krah FAH-mays

greed, greed, greed

Virgil, who knew better than to fall victim to greed, declaiming literally "to what do you not drive mortal hearts, accursed hunger for gold?"

quid prodest?
kwihd PROH-dehst

what good does it do?

quidquid delirant reges, plectuntur Achivi
KWIHD-kwihd day-LEE-rahnt RAY-gays plehk-TUUN-tuur ah-KHEE-wee

whatever folly their rulers commit, the Greeks suffer the penalty

A proverb of Horace that has not lost its cogency over the centuries, suggesting that it's the innocent people who get hurt. **Achivus** (ah-KHEE-wuus) was an ancient term for "Greek." Today, in place of "Greeks" read "Bosnians," "Haitians," or any of a multiplicity of other peoples.

quid rides?
kwihd REE-days

why are you laughing?

quid sit futurum cras, fuge quaerere
kwihd siht fuu-TOO-ruum kraahs FUU-geh KWĪ-reh-reh
live in the here and now

Horace advising us literally to "avoid asking what tomorrow will bring." Nobody will know until tomorrow is today.

quid times?
kwihd TIH-mays
what do you fear?

quid verum atque decens
kwihd WAY-ruum AHT-kweh DEH-kayns
what is true and seemly

Television executives and newscasters, consider this phrase from Horace when planning your programs.

quieta non movere
kwih-YAY-tah nohn maw-WAY-reh
let sleeping dogs lie

Literally "not to disturb quiet things," better translated as "don't disturb things that are at peace." Today some of us are apt to say, "If it ain't broke, don't fix it." (See also NE PRIUS ANTIDOTUM QUAM VENENUM.)

qui facit per alium facit per se
kwee FAH-kiht pehr AH-lih-yuum FAH-kiht pehr say
you cannot shift the blame

This legal principle, literally "one who does a thing through another does it oneself," tells us that we are legally responsible for the actions of our agents. So if someone you hire steals a car for you, you can expect to be charged with the theft yourself.

qui iacet (or jacet) in terra non habet unde cadat
kwee YAH-keht ihn TEHR-raah nohn HAH-beht UUN-deh KAH-daht
nowhere to go but up

This observation, nearly literally "one who lies on the ground has no chance to fall," puts the best face on a desperate situation. John Bunyan, the seventeenth-century English writer and preacher whose pilgrim made considerable progress, put it this way: "He that is down, needs fear no fall."

qui invidet minor est
kwee IHN-wih-deht MIH-nawr ehst
one who envies is the less for it

See also OMNIBUS INVIDEAS, LIVIDE, NEMO TIBI.

qui male agit odit lucem
kwee MAH-lay AH-giht OH-diht LOO-kehm
one who does evil hates daylight

And that's why malefactors shudder at the thought of sunshine laws. (See also EX UMBRA IN SOLEM.)

qui nimium probat nihil probat
kwee NIH-mih-yuum PRAW-baht NIH-hihl PRAW-baht
one who proves too much proves nothing

Stay with the central point you are trying to make. Don't answer questions you have not been asked. And, for the trial lawyer, don't ask an idle question. You don't know what damaging information will be revealed in the answer.

qui non proficit deficit
kwee nohn PROH-fih-kiht DAY-fih-kiht
it's pointless to run in place

More literally "one who does not advance loses ground." This would appear to be the guiding principle of aggressive entrepreneurs. By putting too much faith in this dictum and trying to grow too fast, they may endanger an already successful enterprise.

qui parcit nocentibus innocentes punit
kwee PAHR-kiht naw-KEHN-tih-buus ihn-naw-KEHN-tays POO-niht

an argument for harsh justice

Literally "who spares the guilty punishes the innocent." (For another way of saying the same thing, see BONIS NOCET QUISQUIS PEPERCERIT MALIS.)

qui sentit commodum sentire debet et onus
kwee SEHN-tiht KAWM-maw-duum sehn-TEE-reh DAY-beht eht AW-nuus

there's no such thing as a free lunch

Literally "one who experiences the benefit should experience the burden as well."

quocumque modo
kwoh-KUUM-kweh MAW-doh

in whatever manner

quocumque nomine
kwoh-KUUM-kweh NOH-mih-neh

under whatever name

quod absurdum est
kwawd ahb-SUUR-duum ehst

which thing is absurd

A phrase used to close an argument based on demonstrating that an opponent's position cannot logically be true.

quod bene notandum
kwawd BEH-neh naw-TAHN-duum
which is to be especially noted

A scholarly notation.

quod bonum, felix, faustumque sit!
kwawd BAW-nuum FAY-leeks fows-TUUM-kweh siht
and may it be lucky, prosperous, and auspicious!

Could anyone ask for more? An excellent candidate for inclusion in a toast offered at a wedding celebration.

quod licet Iovi (or Jovi) non licet bovi
kwawd LIH-keht YAW-wee nohn LIH-keht BAW-wee
that which Jove is permitted, an ox is not

Except perhaps for citizens of perfect democracies, we are not all entitled to the same treatment in all matters—Jove was an alternative name for Jupiter, and Jupiter was a very important god. An ox is an ox.

quod minime crederes
kwawd MIH-nih-may KRAY-deh-rays
what one would least suppose

quod non opus est, asse carum est
kwawd nohn AW-puus ehst AHS-seh KAAH-ruum ehst
what is not necessary is dear at a penny

Good to keep in mind when shopping a sale or making one's way through a flea market.

quod sciam
kwawd SKIH-yahm
as far as I know

quod sentimus loquamur, quod loquimur sentiamus

kwawd sehn-TEE-muus law-KWAAH-muur kwawd LAW-kwih-muur sen-tih-AAH-muus

say what you mean, mean what you say

A maxim from Seneca the Younger, literally "let us say what we think, let us understand what we say." For those who study each word in this entry, understand that the verb **sentio** (SEHN-tih-yoh), of which *sentimus* and *sentiamus* are forms, has many meanings.

quod volumus, facile credimus

kwawd WAW-luu-muus FAH-kihh-leh KRAY-dih-muus

we readily believe what we wish to believe

quo fas et gloria ducunt

kwoh faahs eht GLOH-rih-yah DOO-kuunt

where duty and glory lead

quo Fata vocant

kwoh FAAH-tah WAW-kahnt

whither the Fates call

The Romans were fatalistic. When we go *quo Fata vocant*, we avoid taking responsibility for our own actions.

quo pax et gloria ducunt

kwoh paahks eht GLOH-rih-yah DOO-kuunt

where peace and glory lead

quorum pars magna fui

KWOH-ruum pahrs MAHG-nah FUU-wee

of which I was an important part

Aeneas, in Virgil's *Aeneid*, launching his recital to Dido of the disasters that befell the Trojans.

quot servi tot hostes
kwawt SEHR-wee tawt HAWS-tays
watch out especially for the people close to you

Literally "so many servants, so many enemies."

quousque tandem abutere patientia nostra?
kwoh-UUS-kweh TAHN-dehm ahb-oo-TAY-reh pah-tih-YEHN-tih-yaah NAWS-traah
how long will you abuse our patience?

The famous question that Cicero, in an oration before the Roman Senate, addressed to Catiline (Lucius Sergius Catilina), who conspired to plunder the Roman treasury, destroy the Senate, and assassinate the consul, Cicero himself. (See also ALIENI APPETENS.)

R

redintegratio amoris
reh-dihn-teh-GRAAH-tih-yoh ah-MOH-rihs
the renewal of love

redire ad nuces
reh-DEE-reh ahd NUU-kays
to resume childish follies

This expression, literally "to return to the nuts," is the opposite of **relinquere** (reh-LIHN-kweh-reh) **nuces**, "to abandon the nuts." In ancient Rome it was conventional after a wedding for the bridegroom to scatter nuts to the onlookers in the street, to symbolize that he was giving up boyish playthings. Thus, *redire ad nuces* represents a regression from adulthood, much like watching football games on TV all day Sunday while one's spouse steams.

Regina Caeli
ray-GEE-nah KĪ-lee
the Virgin Mary

> Literally "Queen of Heaven."

regium donum
RAY-gih-yuum DOH-nuum
a royal grant *or* a royal gift

regnat populus
RAYG-naht PAW-puu-luus
the people rule

> Motto of Arkansas.

re infecta
ray een-FEHK-taah
unfinished business

> Literally "the matter being unfinished"; also translated as "without achieving one's purpose."

relata refero
reh-LAAH-tah REH-feh-roh
I tell the tale as it was told (to me)

> Don't blame me, I was only the reporter. A way to deny responsibility for an account one gives.

religio loci
reh-LIH-gih-yoh LAW-kee
the sanctity of the place

reliquiae
reh-LIH-kwih-yī
the remains

Of a person who has died, that is. Also translated as "relics."

rem acu tetigisti
rehm AH-koo teh-tih-GIHS-tee
you've hit the nail on the head

Literally "you have touched the thing with a pin." A shortened form of this quotation from Plautus, *rem acu*, is used in archery, meaning "you have hit the bull's-eye." See also TETIGISTI ACU.

remisso animo
reh-MEES-soh AH-nih-moh
listlessly

Literally "with mind relaxed."

rem tene et verba sequentur
rehm TEH-nay eht WEHR-bah seh-KWEHN-tuur
master the material and the words will follow

See also PECTUS EST QUOD DISERTOS FACIT.

renovate animos
reh-naw-WAAH-teh AH-nih-mohs
renew your courage

See also REVOCATE ANIMOS.

repente liberalis stultis gratus est; verum peritis irritos tendit dolos

reh-PEHN-tay lee-beh-RAAH-lihs STUUL-tees GRAAH-tuus ehst WAY-ruum peh-REE-tees IHR-rih-tohs TEHN-diht DAW-lohs

when someone starts giving money away, look out

Wisdom from Plautus, literally "a man who is suddenly generous pleases fools, but he devises futile tricks for the experienced."

repetitio est mater studiorum

reh-peh-TIH-tih-yoh ehst MAAH-tehr stuu-dih-YOH-ruum

repetition is the mother of studies

And that's why homework was born.

rerum primordia

RAY-ruum pree-MAWR-dih-yah

atoms

Literally "the first beginnings of things." The Romans followed the Greeks in seeing atoms as the smallest elements of matter. Today's physicists speak of quarks and other particles much smaller than atoms.

res adversae

rays ahd-WEHR-sī

adversity *or* adverse things

res domesticas noli tangere

rays daw-MEHS-tih-kaahs NOH-lee TAHN-geh-reh

mind your own business

Literally "don't interfere in domestic affairs."

res est ingeniosa dare
rays ehst ihn-geh-nih-YOH-sah DAH-reh
giving requires good sense

Ovid telling us that how and when and to whom one gives are as important as the act of giving itself.

res est sacra miser
rays ehst SAH-krah MIH-sehr
an impoverished person is a sacred object

So be generous in giving charity.

res gestae
rays GEHṢ-tī
facts

Also translated as "things done," "deeds," "exploits," "transactions" and, in law, "the material facts."

res incognitae
rays ihn-KAWG-nih-tī
things unknown *or* matters unknown

res iudicata (or judicata)
rays yoo-dih-KAAH-tah
an adjudicated matter

This phrase is seen in a legal maxim: **res iudicata pro veritate accipitur** (proh way-rih-TAAH-teh ahk-KIH-pih-tuur), literally "a case that has been decided is accepted as truth."

res secundae
rays seh-KUUN-dī
prosperity *or* success

> Literally "favorable things."

revocate animos
reh-waw-KAAH-teh AH-nih-mohs
recover your courage

> See also RENOVATE ANIMOS.

rex convivii
rayks kawn-WEE-wih-yee
king of the feast *or* master of the feast

> Also given as **rex bibendi** (bih-BEHN-dee), literally "king of the drinking," and as **rex vini** (WEE-nee), literally "king of the wine."

rex regnat sed non gubernat
rayks RAYG-naht sehd nohn guu-BEHR-naht
a leader remiss in his duties

> Literally "the king reigns but does not govern."

ridentem dicere verum quid vetat?
ree-DEHN-tehm DEE-keh-reh WAY-ruum kwihd WEH-taht
many a true word is said in jest

> Horace asking literally "what prohibits one from speaking the truth even while laughing?"

ridere in stomacho
ree-DAY-reh ihn STAW-mah-khoh
to laugh up one's sleeve

Literally "to laugh in the stomach *or* in the gullet." We might describe such an action as a belly laugh.

risum teneatis, amici?
REE-suum teh-neh-YAAH-tihs ah-MEE-kee

can this guy be for real?

A rhetorical question from Horace, literally "can you help laughing, my friends?"

rixatur de lana saepe caprina
reeks-AAH-tuur day LAAH-naah SĪ-peh kah-PREE-naah

he (or she) quarrels about nothing

Literally "he (or she) often quarrels about goat's wool." For an explanation of the significance of goat's wool, see DE LANA CAPRINA.

Roma locuta est, causa finita est
ROH-mah law-KOO-tah ehst KOW-sah fee-NEE-tah ehst

that's the end of the matter

Literally "Rome has spoken, the case is ended." The allusion is to the Vatican, or papal authority, which has the final word among Roman Catholics in any discussion of theological principles and practices.

rudis indigestaque moles
RUU-dihs ihn-dee-GEHS-tah-kweh MOH-lays

a chaotic condition

Well translated also as "a formless mass" or more literally as "a rude and undigested mass."

S

saepe creat molles aspera spina rosas
SĪ-peh KREH-yaht MAWL-lays AHS-peh-rah SPEE-nah
RAW-saahs
good things from unexpected sources

Ovid in an expansive but realistic mood, telling us literally "a
sharp thorn often produces delicate roses."

saeva indignatio
SĪ-wah ihn-dihg-NAAH-tih-yoh
fierce indignation

Virgil's phrase.

saevis tranquillus in undis
SĪ-wees trahn-KWIHL-luus ihn UUN-dees
keeping cool when all hell is breaking loose

Literally "calm amid the raging waters." (See also AEQUAM ME-
MENTO REBUS IN ARDUIS SERVARE MENTEM.)

sal sapit omnia
saahl SAH-piht AWM-nih-yah
salt seasons everything

Table salt, sodium chloride, is not intended here. Rather, for
"salt" read "wit" or "sparkling thought well expressed." Now *sal
sapit omnia* cannot be denied. What's better, wouldn't you say,
than good conversation at a meal, no matter how well or poorly
prepared? The food, that is. (See also MERUM SAL.)

salva conscientia
SAHL-waah kohn-skih-YEHN-tih-yah
with a clear conscience

    This phrase can also be translated as "without compromising one's conscience" or, literally, "with conscience intact."

salva dignitate
SAHL-waah dihg-nih-TAAH-teh
without compromising one's dignity

    Literally "with dignity uninjured." And that's the outcome we all hope for after we have taken a beating of one sort or another.

salva fide
SAHL-waah FIH-day
without breaking one's word

    Literally "with one's honor safe."

salva lege
SAHL-waah LAY-geh
without breaking the law

salva res est
SAHL-wah rays ehst
all is well

salva sit reverentia
SAHL-wah siht reh-weh-REHN-tih-yah
let due respect be observed

salvo iure (or jure)
SAHL-woh YOO-reh
without prejudice

A legal term, literally "the right (of someone) being unimpaired."

salvo pudore
SAHL-woh puu-DOH-reh
without shame

salvo sensu
SAHL-woh SAYN-soo
without changing the meaning

This is the challenge faced by translators and editors, to do their work well, literally "without violation of sense."

sapere aude
See AUDE SAPERE.

sapiens dominabitur astris
SAH-pih-yayns daw-mih-NAAH-bih-tuur AHS-trees
the wise man will be master of the stars

That is, he will be master of himself, free of the influence of the stars. As Shakespeare's Cassius said:

> Men at some time are masters of their fates:
> The fault, dear Brutus, is not in our stars,
> But in ourselves, that we are underlings.

sapiens, in se ipso totus, teres atque rotundus
SAH-pih-yayns ihn say IHP-soh TOH-tuus TEH-rehs AHT-kweh raw-TUUN-duus
a wise man, complete in himself, polished and well-rounded

Horace describing someone admirable. How much better can one get? To make this feminine, change it to **sapiens, in se ipsa tota** (IHP-saah TOH-tah), **teres atque rotunda** (raw-TUUN-dah).

sapiens qui prospicit
SAH-pih-yayns kwee PRAWS-pih-kiht
wise is one who looks ahead

sapientem pascere barbam
sah-pih-YEHN-tehm PAAHS-keh-reh BAHR-bahm
to cultivate a wise beard

> If only growing a beard were all it took to become wise.

sat cito si sat bene
saht KIH-taw see saht BEH-neh
fast enough if well enough

sat cito si sat tuto
saht KIH-taw see saht TOO-toh
fast enough if safely enough

satis quod sufficit
SAH-tihs kwawd SUUF-fih-kiht
enough is as good as a feast

> A plug for moderation, literally "what suffices is enough." A spoonful of caviar, not a bowlful; a slice or two of pizza, not the entire pie.

sat pulchra si sat bona
saht PUUL-khrah see saht BAW-nah
handsome is as handsome does

> Literally "beautiful enough if she is good enough." One's actions count for more than one's looks, they say. To make this masculine, change it to **sat pulcher** (PUUL-khehr) **si sat bonus** (BAW-nuus).

scala caeli
SKAH-lah KĪ-lee
ladder to heaven *or* staircase to heaven

scelere velandum est scelus
SKEH-leh-reh way-LAHN-duum ehst SKEH-luus
one misstep leads to another

Irrefutable wisdom from Seneca the Younger, literally "crime must be covered up by crime." (For what Terence had to say along the same lines, see FALLACIA ALIA ALIAM TRUDIT.)

schola cantorum
SKHAW-lah kahn-TOH-ruum
school of singers

scienter
skih-YEHN-tehr
expertly

While the translation above is accurate, when the term appears in a legal context a better translation is "knowingly" or "willfully."

scio cui credidi
SKIH-yoh koowee KRAY-dih-dee
I know whom I have trusted

The credo of the careful credit manager.

scire quid valeant humeri, quid ferre recusent
SKEE-reh kwihd WAH-leh-yahnt HUU-meh-ree kwihd FEHR-reh reh-KOO-sehnt
to know one's limitations

Nearly literally "to know what one's shoulders can carry, what they refuse to carry." The intent here goes beyond burdens literally borne on one's shoulders to debts, demanding studies, work schedules, and all the rest of the demands put on people all through their lives.

scribendi recte sapere est et principium et fons
skree-BEHN-dee RAYK-tay SAH-peh-reh ehst eht preen-KIH-pih-yuum eht fohns
to be a writer, you must have something to say

Horace giving us the first step in becoming a writer, literally "knowledge is the foundation and source of good writing." (See also SCRIBIMUS INDOCTI DOCTIQUE POEMATA PASSIM to see what Horace had to say about poets and would-be poets.)

scribere iussit (or jussit) amor
SKREE-beh-reh YUUS-siht AH-mawr
you drove me to verse

Ovid explaining why he felt impelled to write, literally "love commanded me to write." He was speaking of writing poetry, not love letters.

scribimus indocti doctique poemata passim
SKREE-bih-muus ihn-DAWK-tee dawk-TEE-kweh paw-way-MAAH-tah PAHS-sihm
everybody wants to get into the act

Horace, vexed with untalented amateur versifiers, sounding off in "learned and unlearned, we all write poems indiscriminately."

scriptorum chorus omnis amat nemus et fugit urbem
skreep-TOH-ruum KHAW-ruus AWM-nihs AH-maht NEH-muus eht FUU-giht UUR-behm
find a place in Vermont to do your best writing

Horace, observing contemporary demographic trends in his day, tells us "the whole band of writers loves the woods and flees the city." Things haven't changed much since then, and today we see much good writing emanating from cabins in the woods. So long as there is a good Internet connection.

secundum artem
seh-KUUN-duum AHR-tehm
according to the rules of art

secundum ipsius naturam
seh-KUUN-duum ihp-SEE-yuus naah-TOO-rahm
according to its very nature

secundum legem
seh-KUUN-duum LAY-gehm
according to law

secundum usum
seh-KUUN-duum OOS-uum
according to custom *or* according to usage

The way we generally conduct our speech and ourselves. Or hope to.

secundum veritatem
seh-KUUN-duum way-rih-TAAH-tehm
universally valid

Literally "according to truth."

se defendendo
say day-fehn-DEHN-doh
in self-defense

Literally "in defending oneself."

sede vacante
SAY-deh wah-KAHN-teh
the seat being vacant

The seat here is the bishop's, called also the see, but *sede vacante* now is also applicable to any position ordinarily designated a seat, for example, a Congressional seat.

sed haec hactenus
sehd hīk HAHK-teh-nuus
but so much for this

A good way to close out a topic under discussion in order to turn to another topic. (See also AD MELIORA VERTAMUR.)

seditio civium hostium est occasio
say-DIH-tih-yoh KEE-wih-yuum HAWS-tih-yuum ehst awk-KAAH-sih-yoh
keep people content and quiet

A lesson in governing, literally "civil discord is the enemy's opportunity." The enemy may be the political party out of power at home as well as a foreign power with the capacity and inclination to mount a military attack.

semel abbas, semper abbas
SEH-mehl AHB-baahs SEHM-pehr AHB-baahs
once an abbot, always an abbot

It takes more than an abandonment of ecclesiastical habit or a change of vocation to alter anyone's strongly held beliefs.

semel pro semper
SEH-mehl proh SEHM-pehr
once for always

semper avarus eget
SEHM-pehr ah-WAAH-ruus EH-geht

avarice is never satisfied

Horace telling us "a greedy man is always in need." (See also DESUNT INOPIAE MULTA, AVARITIAE OMNIA.)

semper et ubique
SEHM-pehr eht uu-BEE-kweh

always and everywhere

semper felix
SEHM-pehr FAY-leeks

always fortunate *or* always successful

semper timidum scelus
SEHM-pehr TIH-mih-duum SKEH-luus

crime is always fearful

The guilty live in fear of being found out.

senatus consultum
seh-NAAH-toos kohn-SUUL-tuum

a decree of the senate

The senate of ancient Rome, of course. The U.S. Senate is not empowered to issue decrees. The courts do that.

senectus insanabilis morbus est
seh-NEHK-toos een-saah-NAAH-bih-lihs MAWR-buus ehst

old age is an incurable disease

But usually considered to be better than dying.

senex bis puer

See BIS PUERI SENES.

sensu bono
SAYN-soo BAW-noh
in a good sense

sensu malo
SAYN-soo MAH-loh
in a bad sense

sequiturque patrem non passibus aequis
seh-kwih-TUUR-kweh PAH-trehm nohn PAHS-sih-buus
Ī-kwees
he's no match for his father

Virgil, speaking of the young son of Aeneas, gave us a metaphor we can apply to any son of any father, literally "he follows
his father, but not with equal steps." We all know, of course,
that in many father-son combinations the younger member far
outstrips the elder. (See also HAUD PASSIBUS AEQUIS.)

sequor non inferior
SEH-kwawr nohn een-FEH-rih-yawr
I follow but I am not inferior

Makes for good labor-management relations. Especially in a
democracy.

serus in caelum redeas
SAY-ruus ihn KĪ-luum REH-deh-yaahs
may you live long!

Horace addressed Augustus, his emperor, in these words, literally "late may you return to heaven," giving us an appropriate
toast—but one always to be given in Latin. The literal English

translation does not sit as well as the conventional toast given above. People usually want to live long, but they don't want to be reminded that somewhere along the line they will be going to their so-called great reward.

servabo fidem
sehr-WAAH-boh FIH-dehm
I will keep the faith

sic eunt fata hominum
seek EH-yuunt FAAH-tah HAW-mih-nuum
thus go the destinies of men

sic me servavit Apollo
seek may sehr-WAAH-wiht ah-PAWL-loh
thus Apollo preserved me

Presumably to accomplish great deeds. Horace, referring to the Greek god of, among other things, prophecy, music, medicine, archery, and the sun.

sic passim
seek PAHS-sihm
so here and there throughout

A scholarly phrase intended to direct the reader's attention to the appearance in a text of a particular topic or topics identified by the writer. Sometimes just the word *passim* is used.

sicut meus est mos
SEEK-uut MEH-yuus ehst mohs
as is my habit

sic volo sic iubeo (or jubeo)
seek WAW-loh seek YUU-beh-yoh
thus I will, thus I command

Juvenal, giving you a way to make clear that you have every intention of getting your own way.

si fortuna iuvat (or juvat)
see fohr-TOO-nah YUU-waht
if fortune favors

si hic esses, aliter sentires
see heek EHS-says AH-lih-tehr sehn-TEE-rays
if you were here, you would think otherwise

The rejoinder available when a person who lacks pertinent practical knowledge offers an opinion. Consider, for example, those who claim that staying at home to raise children is easier than working at a traditional job. Simply say to that person, *Si hic esses, aliter sentires.*

sile et philosophus esto
SIH-lay eht phih-LAW-saw-phuus EHS-toh
hold your tongue and you will pass for a philosopher

Literally "be silent and be a philosopher," freely rendered as "be quiet, and people will think you're wise."

silentium altum
sih-LEHN-tih-yuum AHL-tuum
profound silence

simile simili gaudet
SIH-mih-leh SIH-mih-lee GOW-deht
birds of a feather flock together

Literally "like delights in like."

similiter
sih-MIH-lih-tehr
similarly *or* in like manner

simplex munditiis
SIHM-pleks muun-DIH-tih-yees
elegant in simplicity

Horace, who knew how to butter people up, used this phrase, literally "natural in (your) elegance," in addressing a beautiful woman. Clearly, in her case, less was more for Horace.

simpliciter
sihm-PLIH-kih-tehr
simply

But also well translated as "naturally," "frankly," "without reserve," and "absolutely."

simul sorbere ac flare non possum
SIH-muul sawr-BAY-reh ahk FLAAH-reh nohn PAWS-suum
make up your mind—one way or the other

This homely truth is well translated as "I cannot simultaneously exhale and inhale," more literally as "I cannot swallow and blow at the same time." This expression may be used to tell an ambivalent person to clarify an instruction. It is especially apposite when the driver of a car is told by a pair of backseat drivers to turn both left and right at the next traffic light.

sine anno
SIH-neh AHN-noh
undated

A scholarly notation, literally "without a year," indicating that a cited source carries no reliable date of composition or publication.

sine Cerere et Libero friget Venus
SIH-neh KEH-reh-reh eht LEE-beh-roh FREE-geht WEH-nuus

love dies on an empty stomach

A realistic adage of Terence that has its charm. Ceres (whose name gives us the English word *cereal*) was a goddess of agriculture, Liber a god of wine and vineyards, and Venus a goddess of love. Terence, thus, was telling us literally that "Venus grows cold without Ceres and Liber," more conventionally that "love grows cold without bread and wine."

sine cortice natare
SIH-neh KAWR-tih-keh nah-TAAH-reh

to need no assistance

Literally "to swim (or float) without cork."

sine dolo malo
SIH-neh DAW-loh MAH-loh

without deceit

Also translated as "without fraud" and "without evil intent."

sine ictu
SIH-neh IHK-too

without a blow *or* without a wound

The amicable way to settle a dispute.

sine ioco (or joco)
SIH-neh YAW-koh

seriously

Literally "without jest."

sine ira et studio
SIH-neh EE-raah eht STUU-dih-yoh
calmly and fairly

A phrase from Tacitus, literally "without anger and partiality."

sine macula et ruga
SIH-neh MAH-kuu-laah eht ROO-gaah
without stain or wrinkle

In one's reputation, that is. But also the way we want our clothes to come back from the dry cleaner.

sine nomine vulgus
SIH-neh NOH-mih-neh WUUL-guus
the multitude without a name

An arrogant characterization of ordinary people.

sine pennis volare haud facile est
SIH-neh PEHN-nees waw-LAAH-reh howd FAH-kih-leh ehst
don't try anything you're not ready for

Plautus offering excellent advice, literally "it's not at all easy to fly without wings." Implicit in this statement is encouragement to prepare oneself for new challenges. But consider the legend of Icarus and his father, Daedalus, who were able to flee imprisonment by Minos, king of Crete, on wings built by Daedalus. Unfortunately, Icarus flew so close to the sun that the wax attaching feathers to his wings melted and he fell into the sea. So we are encouraged by this story not to attempt more than we are able to accomplish.

sine prole superstite
SIH-neh PRO-leh suu-PEHR-stih-teh
without surviving offspring

A legal term.

si peccavi, insciens feci
see pehk-KAAH-wee EEN-skih-yayns FAY-kee
how to claim innocence when guilty

Terence telling us what to say when we're caught red-handed, literally "If I made a mistake, I did so unwittingly."

si vis ad summum progredi, ab infimo ordire
see wees ahd SUUM-muum proh-GREH-dee ahb EEN-fih-moh awr-DEE-reh
don't expect too much all at once

Good advice, literally "if you want to reach the top, start at the bottom." Unless one of your relatives owns the business.

si vis amari ama
see wees ah-MAAH-ree AH-maah
love is a two-way street

Seneca the Younger offering sound advice to the loveless, "if you want to be loved, love." (See also AMOR GIGNIT AMOREM.)

sola nobilitas virtus
SOH-lah noh-BIH-lih-taahs WIHR-toos
virtue is the only nobility

For an amplified phrase, see NOBILITAS SOLA EST ATQUE UNICE VIRTUS.

spargere voces in vulgum ambiguas
SPAHR-geh-reh WOH-kays ihn WUUL-guum ahm-BIH-guu-waahs
how to win elections

Virgil defining the art of propagandizing, literally "to spread equivocal rumor among the multitude."

spectemur agendo
spehk-TAY-muur ah-GEHN-doh
let us be judged by our actions

Not by hearsay or how we dress, for example.

spem pretio non emo
spehm PREH-tih-yoh nohn EH-moh
don't try to sell me expectations

Terence, ever the realist, telling us "I do not pay money for mere hope."

sperate miseri, cavete felices
spay-RAAH-teh MIH-seh-ree kah-WAY-teh fay-LEE-kays
you never know the card you will be dealt next

This maxim, literally "hope, you wretched persons; beware, you successful people," offers valuable advice. Just when life looks bleakest, all may not be lost; just when everything seems to be going your way, you may stumble. For reinforcement of this advice, see also SPERAT INFESTIS, METUIT SECUNDIS.

sperat infestis, metuit secundis
SPAY-raht een-FEHS-tees MEH-tuu-wiht seh-KUUN-dees
your present situation is not cast in concrete

Horace, speaking approvingly of the person who does not take the future for granted, tells us literally "he hopes in dangerous times and fears in times of good fortune." (See also SPERATE MISERI, CAVETE FELICES.)

spes sibi quisque
spays SIH-bih KWIHS-kweh
rely on yourself

Virgil telling us not to depend on others, "let each be his own hope."

spicula et faces amoris
SPEE-kuu-lah eht FAH-kays ah-MOH-rihs
love's artillery

If we are to take at face value this phrase, literally "the darts and torches of love," love stings and burns. Fortunately, people seem to be able to withstand such suffering.

splendide mendax
SPLEHN-dih-day MEHN-daahks
untruthful for good purpose

This brilliant phrase from Horace—one meaning of *splendide* is "brilliantly"—here carries the literal meaning of "nobly untruthful." It is surely applicable to many situations in life, of greater and lesser importance, in which diplomats and spouses, for example, consider a bit of mendacity to be the better part of wisdom.

spretae iniuria (or injuria) formae
SPRAY-tī ihn-YOO-rih-yah FAWR-mī
the insult of slighted beauty

This phrase from Virgil's *Aeneid* teaches us how much trouble can result from beauty scorned. The story involving beauty scorned began when Paris was chosen to be the judge in the mother of all beauty contests—only three entrants, all of them goddesses: Hera (Juno), Athene (Minerva), and Aphrodite (Venus). Aphrodite promised Paris that if he chose her, she would reward him with the hand of the most beautiful woman in the world. Aphrodite won, of course, and as sure as night follows day, Hera never forgave Paris. This was *spretae iniuria formae*. But the story is not over. Whom did Paris win as his reward from Aphrodite? Helen of Troy. Unfortunately, Helen was already married to the king of Sparta, and when Paris ran off with Helen, there was launched the devastating Trojan War—in which Paris lost his life. So Helen's face may have "launched a thousand ships," in Christopher Marlowe's phrase, but it also "burnt the topless towers of Ilium," again Marlowe's phrase. The moral? It does not pay to slight a vindictive goddess. Especially a beautiful one. (See also TAETERRIMA BELLI CAUSA.)

stant belli causae
stahnt BEHL-lee KOW-sī
the causes of war remain

A phrase from Virgil indicating that wars do not settle anything when their outcomes do not repair the unhappy circumstances that led to the wars.

stare decisis, et non quieta movere
STAAH-reh day-KEE-sees eht nohn kwih-YAY-tah maw-WAY-reh
to uphold legal precedents

A phrase often abbreviated in our appellate courts as the principle of "*stare decisis*," in English pronounced STAIR-ee dih-SĪ-sis, "let the precedent stand." The full Latin phrase may be translated as "to stand by things decided, and not to disturb settled issues."

stare super vias antiquas
STAAH-reh SUU-pehr WIH-yaahs ahn-TEE-kwaahs
to cling to the old ways

Literally "to stand upon the ancient ways," also translated as "to be conservative."

stat fortuna domus virtute
staht fawr-TOO-nah DAW-moos wihr-TOO-teh
everything depends on having a good reputation

Literally "the success of the house stands by its virtue." A good motto for commercial enterprises that expect to endure for generations.

stat magni nominis umbra

See NOMINIS UMBRA.

stemmata quid faciunt?
STEHM-mah-tah kwihd FAH-kih-yuunt
you say your family arrived on the Mayflower?

Juvenal giving us what self-made men and the upwardly mobile would consider a splendid rhetorical question, literally "of what value are pedigrees?" But Juvenal did go on to supply a Roman answer. See NOBILITAS SOLA EST ATQUE UNICE VIRTUS.

stilus virum arguit
STIH-luus WIH-ruum AHR-guu-wiht
the style proves the man

A comment on the uniqueness of rhetorical style. Best known to most of us in the French adage *le style c'est l'homme même*, "the style is the man himself." Count de Buffon, an eighteenth-century naturalist, spoke these words in his address upon the occasion of his reception into the French Academy.

strenua inertia
STRAY-nuu-wah ih-NEHR-tih-yah
energetic idleness

A wonderful oxymoron from Horace, telling us that it often takes a lot of work to appear to keep busy doing nothing. (See also OTIOSA SEDULITAS.)

stricto sensu
STRIHK-toh SAYN-soo
in a strict sense

> The opposite of LATO SENSU.

studium immane loquendi
STUU-dih-yuum ihm-MAAH-neh law-KWEHN-dee
a prodigious fondness for talking

> Ovid's polite term. More often described as **furor** (FUU-rawr) **loquendi**, "a rage for speaking."

stultum facit fortuna quem vult perdere
STUUL-tuum FAH-kiht fohr-TOO-nah kwehm wuult PEHR-deh-reh
Dame Fortune first makes a fool out of the man she wishes to destroy

> A proverb from Publilius Syrus. Beware, all you wealthy men of advanced age seeking a beautiful wife of twenty-five. Or less.

sua munera mittit cum hamo
SUU-wah MUU-neh-rah MIHT-tiht kuum HAAH-moh
a sprat to catch a whale

> This saying, literally "he (or she) sends gifts with a hook attached," suggests a person who makes a concession in the hope of a bigger return. A chess player's gambit is an example of this cunning.

sua si bona norint
SUU-wah see BAW-nah NOH-rihnt
if they but knew their blessings

> A phrase from Virgil. For the full statement see O FORTUNATOS NIMIUM, SUA SI BONA NORINT!

suave, mari magno turbantibus aequora ventis, e terra magnum alterius spectare laborem

SWAAH-weh MAH-ree MAHG-noh tuur-BAHN-tih-buus
Ī-kwaw-rah WEHN-tees ay TEHR-raah MAHG-nuum ahl-
teh-REE-yuus spehk-TAAH-reh lah-BOH-rehm

it's easy to shout "kill him" from ringside

Sardonic wisdom from Lucretius, literally "it's pleasant when safe on land to watch the great struggle of another out on a swelling sea, amid winds churning the deep."

sublata causa tollitur effectus

suub-LAAH-taah KOW-saah TAWL-lih-tuur ehf-FEHK-
tuus

a real cure

Literally "once the cause is removed, the effect disappears."

sub specie

suub SPEH-kih-yay

under the appearance of *or* under the pretext of

sume superbiam quaesitam meritis

SOO-meh suu-PEHR-bih-yahm kwī-SEE-tahm MEH-rih-
tees

take satisfaction in your accomplishments

Horace telling us literally "assume the pride earned by your good deeds."

summo studio

SUUM-moh STUU-dih-yoh

with the greatest zeal

sumptibus publicis
SUUMP-tih-buus POO-blih-kees

at public expense

Congressional junkets are made *sumptibus publicis.*

sum quod eris, fui quod sis
suum kwawd EH-rihs FUU-wee kwawd sees

I am what you will be, I was what you are

An intentionally chilling Roman tombstone inscription.

sunt bona, sunt quaedam mediocria, sunt mala plura
suunt BAW-nah suunt KWĪ-dahm meh-dih-YAW-krih-yah suunt MAH-lah PLOO-rah

some things are good, some middling, but more are bad

Martial, skewing the normal curve of distribution.

sunt lacrimae rerum
suunt LAH-krih-mī RAY-ruum

human lives are not free of sorrow

Virgil telling us literally "there are tears for things (that have happened)."

suo Marte
SUU-woh MAAHR-teh

by one's own exertions

Mars (maahrs) is known especially as the Roman god of war, but he was also the patron of farmers—who work hard and must be prudent managers—and typified divine fortitude.

suo periculo

SUU-woh peh-REE-kuu-loh

at one's own peril

suo sibi gladio hunc iugulo (or jugulo)

SUU-woh SIH-bih GLAH-dih-yoh huunk YUU-guu-loh

I'll use this man's own words against him

Terence telling us literally "I will cut this man's throat with his own sword."

superstitione tollenda religio non tollitur

suu-pehr-stih-tih-YOH-neh tawl-LEHN-dah reh-LIH-gih-yoh nohn TAWL-lih-tuur

religion is not abolished by eliminating superstition

Cicero's observation on the durability of religion. Indeed, the British politician and man of letters Edmund Burke (1729–1797) gave us this aphorism, "Religion, not atheism, is the true remedy for superstition."

suppressio veri, suggestio falsi

suup-PREHS-sih-yoh WAY-ree suug-GEHS-tih-yoh FAHL-see

suppression of truth is suggestion of falsehood

Press spokespersons, beware.

surgit amari aliquid quod in ipsis floribus angat

SUUR-giht ah-MAAH-ree AH-lih-kwihd kwawd ihn IHP-sees FLOH-rih-buus AHN-gaht

there's always a fly in the ointment

Lucretius telling us literally "something bitter always arises to bring torment amid the very flowers."

suspendens omnia naso
suus-PEHN-dayns AWM-nih-yah NAAH-soh
sneering at everything

Horace characterizing a finicky person, literally "turning up the nose at everything." See also OMNIA SUSPENDENS NASO.

suspensio per collum
suus-PEHN-sih-yoh pehr KAWL-luum
a necktie party

Less colloquially, "execution by hanging." Literally, "suspension by the neck."

suspiria de profundis
suus-PEE-rih-yah day praw-FUUN-dees
sighs from the depths

Of the soul, that is.

suum cuique
SUU-wuum KOOWEE-kweh
to each his (or her) own

T

tacitae magis et occultae inimicitiae timendae sunt quam indictae atque apertae
TAH-kih-tī MAH-gihs eht awk-KUUL-tī ihn-ih-mee-KIH-tih-yī tih-MEHN-dī suunt kwahm ihn-DIHK-tī AHT-kweh ah-PEHR-tī
it's hard to deal with closet enemies

Cicero, an astute political leader, reflecting on foes he faced, tells us literally that "silent, hidden enmities are more to be feared than those that are openly expressed."

tacitum vivit sub pectore vulnus
TAH-kih-tuum WEE-wiht suub PEHK-taw-reh WUUL-nuus

a wound unuttered lives deep within the breast

Virgil, centuries before Freud, giving us this helpful insight: It's better not to suffer personal attacks in silence. Or is it?

taeterrima belli causa
tī-TEHR-rih-mah BEHL-lee KOW-sah

the most repulsive cause of war

A powerful characterization by Horace. And what was that cause? Abduction of a woman, Helen of Troy. And how did the ten-year Trojan War turn out? Troy was sacked and burned. (See also SPRETAE INIURIA FORMAE.)

tam Marte quam Mercurio
tahm MAAHR-teh kwahm mehr-KUU-rih-yoh

as much by fighting as by business

Literally "as much by Mars as by Mercury." Mercury was the Roman god of trade. It is interesting to note that, among other hats that Mercury wore, he was also the god of thieves. (See also TAM MARTE QUAM MINERVA.)

tam Marte quam Minerva
tahm MAAHR-teh kwahm mih-NEHR-wah

as much by fighting as by wisdom

Literally "as much by Mars as by Minerva." Mars was the Roman god of war, Minerva the Roman goddess of wisdom. (See also TAM MARTE QUAM MERCURIO.)

tamquam in speculum
TAHM-kwahm ihn SPEH-kuu-luum

as in a mirror

Examine yourself and your motives. (See also VELUTI IN SPE-CULUM.)

tandem fit surculus arbor
TAHN-dehm fiht SUUR-kuu-luus AHR-bawr
don't be impatient—they'll grow up

Comfort for parents, literally "a twig at length becomes a tree." (See also PARVIS E GLANDIBUS QUERCUS.)

tantaene animis caelestibus irae?
tahn-TĪ-neh AH-nih-mees kī-LEHS-tih-buus EE-rī
can heavenly minds yield to such rage?

Virgil remarking on anger shown by the gods.

tantas componere lites
TAHN-taahs kawm-POH-neh-reh LEE-tays
to settle such great disputes

tantum religio potuit suadere malorum
TAHN-tuum reh-LIH-gih-yoh PAW-tuu-wiht swaah-DAY-reh mah-LOH-ruum
the effects of religion are not always benign

Homer related that Agamemnon commanded the Greek forces in the invasion of Troy. When Agamemnon's fleet was becalmed en route to Troy, he was willing to offer his daughter Iphigenia as a sacrifice to the goddess Artemis, a huntress. It was this intention that provoked Lucretius to remark *tantum religio potuit suadere malorum*, literally "for so many evils has religion been responsible," more elegantly translated as "such evil deeds could religion prompt." Incidentally, in some accounts Artemis snatched Iphigenia away before her father could carry out the bloody deed, and when Agamemnon returned from Troy he was himself murdered by his wife Clytemnestra and her lover Aegisthus.

tantus amor scribendi
TAHN-tuus AH-mawr skree-BEHN-dee
such a passion for writing

Horace on writers—talented or otherwise—who never give up.

tecum habita, noris quam sit tibi curta supellex
TAY-kuum HAH-bih-taah NOH-rihs kwahm siht TIH-bih KUUR-tah suu-PEHL-lehks
realize how much you have still to learn

Persius telling us literally "dwell within yourself, you will know how incomplete is your mental furniture."

te hominem esse memento
tay HAW-mih-nehm EHS-seh meh-MEHN-toh
remember you are a human being

And nothing more.

tempore felici multi numerantur amici
TEHM-paw-reh fay-LEE-kee MUUL-tee nuu-meh-RAHN-tuur ah-MEE-kee
people flock to the sides of the powerful

Hackneyed but true, nearly literally "we can count many friends when we are successful." Also given as **felicitas habet multos amicos** (fay-LEE-kih-taahs HAH-beht MUUL-tohs ah-MEE-kohs), "prosperity has many friends." (See also UBI AMICI, IBI OPES.)

tempus omnia revelat
TEHM-puus AWM-nih-ya reh-WAY-laht
time reveals everything

tenax et fidelis
TEH-naahks eht fih-DAY-lihs
steadfast and faithful

tentanda via est
ten-TAHN-dah WIH-yah ehst
the way must be tried

Virgil urging us not to give up easily, but to explore any method that shows promise.

terminus ad quem
TEHR-mih-nuus ahd kwehm
a destination

Literally "the end toward which."

terminus ante quem
TEHR-mih-nuus AHN-teh kwehm
a point in time before which

More comprehensibly translated as "an established date or time before which an event must have occurred." (See also TER-MINUS POST QUEM.)

terminus post quem
TEHR-mih-nuus pawst kwehm
a point in time after which

More comprehensibly translated as "an established date or time after which an event must have occurred." (See also TERMI-NUS ANTE QUEM.)

terrae filius
TEHR-rī FEE-lih-yuus
a peasant

Literally "a son of the soil."

terras irradient
TEHR-raahs ihr-RAH-dih-yehnt
may they illumine the earth

> Motto of Amherst College.

tetigisti acu
teh-tih-GIHS-tee AH-koo
you've hit the nail on the head

> A phrase from Plautus, literally "you have touched it with a needle." (See also REM ACU TETIGISTI.)

tibi seris, tibi metis
TIH-bih SEHH-rihs TIH-bih MEH-tihs

> I am the master of my fate;
> I am the captain of my soul.

> In these lines from "Invictus," William Ernest Henley tells people that they have individual responsibility for the lives they lead—in the Latin phrase, literally "you sow for yourself, you reap for yourself." (See also UT SEMENTEM FECERIS, ITA METES and AT SPES NON FRACTA.)

time Deum, cole regem
TIH-may DEH-yuum KAW-leh RAY-gehm
fear God, honor the king

> A worthwhile distinction.

timet pudorem
TIH-meht puu-DOH-rehm
he (or she) fears shame

> Also translated as "he (or she) fears disgrace."

timidi mater non flet
TIH-mih-dee MAAH-tehr nohn fleht
think of your mother and don't take undue risks

Probably intended sardonically, since this advice, literally "the mother of a timid man does not weep," is not what we would expect from Romans.

timor belli
TIH-mawr BEHL-lee
fear of war

timor fecit deos
TIH-mawr FAY-kiht DEH-yohs
fear, all-powerful fear

When faced with awesome and unexplainable natural phenomena, the ancients sought supernatural explanations, giving us this phrase, literally "fear created the gods." And throughout time, many soldiers in the grip of fear have been known to call on God to protect them. (See also IN VOTA MISEROS ULTIMUS COGIT TIMOR.)

timor mortis morte peior (or pejor)
TIH-mawr MAWR-tihs MAWR-teh PAY-yawr
fear of death is worse than death

Perhaps.

toto caelo errare
TOH-toh KĪ-loh ehr-RAAH-reh
to be greatly mistaken

Literally "to err by the entire heaven." Talk about being off the mark!

trahimur omnes studio laudis, et optimus quisque maxime gloria ducitur

TRAH-hih-muur AWM-nays STUU-dih-yoh LOW-
dihs eht AWP-tih-muus KWIHS-kweh MAHKS-ih-may
GLOH-rih-yaah DOO-kih-tuur

how we are misled by our yearning for fame

Cicero speaking to all of us past and present who have ex-
hibited an inordinate desire to achieve fame, literally "we are
all impelled by a desire to be praised, and the higher a man's
standing, the more he is deceived by glory."

trahit sua quemque voluptas

TRAH-hiht SUU-wah KWEHM-kweh waw-LUUP-taahs

we all have our own quirks

Virgil reminding us literally that "his (or her) own pleasure
draws each person."

tristis eris si solus eris

TRIHS-tihs EH-rihs see SOH-luus EH-rihs

you will be sad if you remain alone

Ovid encouraging us to take a mate—or at least a close
friend.

truditur dies die

TROO-dih-tuur DIH-yays DIH-yay

days on end

Horace commenting on the tedium of life, literally "a day is
pushed onward by a day," better translated as "one day follows
on the heels of another."

tu enim, Caesar, civitatem dare potes hominibus, verba non potes

See CAESAR NON SUPRA GRAMMATICOS.

u

ubi amici, ibi opes
UU-bee ah-MEE-kee IH-bee AW-pays
where there are friends, there is wealth

Suggesting unfortunately that too many people seek out the company of the wealthy.

ubi ius (or **jus**), **ibi officium**
UU-bee yoos IH-bee awf-FIH-kih-yuum
privilege does not come free

Literally "where there is a right, there is also a duty."

ubi ius (or **jus**), **ibi remedium**
UU-bee yoos IH-bee reh-MEH-dih-yuum
where law prevails, there is a remedy

For every injustice, that is.

ubi ius (or **jus**) **incertum, ibi ius** (or **jus**) **nullum**
UU-bee yoos ihn-KEHR-tuum IH-bee yoos NOOL-luum
uncertainty destroys law

Literally "where the law is uncertain, there is no law." When carried to an extreme, the result is anarchy—essentially no law.

ubi panis, ibi patria
UU-bee PAAH-nihs IH-bee PAH-trih-yah
above all, I must eat

The motto, literally "wherever there is bread, there is my country," of people in desperate economic circumstances who are intent on fleeing their homeland to seek a better life.

ultimus Romanorum
OOL-tih-muus roh-maah-NOH-ruum
the last of the Romans

This title pays tribute to personal character and achievement as well as implying recognition of the contributions ancient Rome made to Western civilization. "The last of the Romans" has been attached to a number of historical and literary personages, including Brutus (Marcus Junius Brutus)—the famed Roman senator and leader in the assassination of Julius Caesar—William Congreve, Samuel Johnson, and Horace Walpole. The title, whether in Latin or in English, has fallen into disuse in recent times.

ultra posse nemo obligatur
OOL-traah PAWS-seh NAY-moh awb-lih-GAAH-tuur
don't bite off more than you can chew

Good advice, literally "no one is obliged to do more than he (or she) can."

una et eadem persona
OO-nah eht eh-YAH-dehm pehr-SOH-nah
one and the same person

uni aequus virtuti, atque eius amicis
OO-nee Ī-kwuus wihr-TOO-tee AHT-kweh EH-yuus ah-MEE-kees
well-disposed to virtue alone and to its friends

A phrase from Horace suggesting that virtue is the motivator underlying the activities and beliefs of good people. Nothing else counts for as much.

unica virtus necessaria
OO-nih-kah WIHR-toos neh-kehs-SAAH-rih-yah
virtue is the only thing necessary

uni navi ne committas omnia
OO-nee NAAH-wee nay kawm-MIHT-taahs AWM-nih-yah

don't put all your eggs in one basket

A Roman metaphor, literally "don't commit everything (you own) to one ship," advising us to act prudently in any project we undertake—especially when investing for retirement income.

unius dementia dementes efficit multos
oo-NEE-yuus day-MEHN-tih-yah day-MEHN-tays EHF-fih-kiht MUUL-tohs

insanity is catching

Literally "the madness of one person drives many mad." Particularly when that person holds a position of leadership.

uno animo
OO-noh AH-nih-moh

unanimously

Literally "with *or* of one mind."

uno ictu
OO-noh IHK-too

at a single blow

uno saltu
OO-noh SAHL-too

at a single leap

unum post aliud
OO-nuum pawst AH-lih-yuud

one thing at a time

Literally "one thing after another."

urbem latericiam invenit, marmoream reliquit
UUR-behm lah-teh-RIH-kih-yahm ihn-WAY-niht mahr-
MAW-reh-yahm reh-LEE-kwiht

he found the city brick and left it marble

With these words Suetonius was praising Caesar Augustus (63 B.C.–A.D. 14), the grand-nephew and adopted son of Julius Caesar and the first Roman emperor. After Julius Caesar's assassination, Augustus completed many of Caesar's unfinished urban building projects and added many improvements of his own. Suetonius's observation, therefore, is a sincere tribute to Augustus and his architectural achievements. Augustus was noted for his patronage of the arts, and in his reign Latin literature flourished. Indeed, the Augustan Age is considered the golden age of Latin literature.

usque ad satietatem
UUS-kweh ahd sah-tih-yeh-TAAH-tehm

even to the point of satiety

This is how to describe your condition when you've had more than enough—of anything.

usus est optimus magister
OO-suus ehst AWP-tih-muus mah-GIHS-tehr

experience is the best teacher

See also EXPERIENTIA DOCET and USUS TE PLURA DOCEBIT.

usus est tyrannus
OO-suus ehst tü-RAHN-nuus

custom is a tyrant

usus te plura docebit
OO-suus tay PLOO-rah daw-KAY-biht

experience will teach you many things

See also EXPERIENTIA DOCET and USUS EST OPTIMUS MAGISTER.

ut ameris, amabilis esto
uut ah-MAY-rihs ah-MAAH-bih-lihs EHS-toh
how can you be loved if you are not lovable?

Ovid giving sound advice, literally "that you may be loved, be lovable." (See also AMOR GIGNIT AMOREM and SI VIS AMARI AMA.)

ut homo est, ita morem geras
uut HAW-moh ehst IH-tah MOH-rehm GEH-raahs
a prescription for tolerance

Terence giving us good advice for getting along with other people, literally "as a person is, so should your conduct be," or "suit your conduct to the person."

utinam noster esset
UU-tih-nahm NAWS-tehr EHS-seht
we want him (or her) on our side

Literally "would that he (or she) were ours."

ut pignus amicitiae
uut PIHG-nuus ah-mee-KIH-tih-yī
as a token of friendship

ut sementem feceris, ita metes
uut say-MEHN-tehm FAY-keh-rihs IH-tah MEH-tays
as you sow, so shall you reap

See also TIBI SERIS, TIBI METIS.

ut tamquam scopulum sic fugias insolens verbum
uut TAHM-kwahm SKAW-puu-luum seek FUU-gih-yaahs
EEN-saw-layns WEHR-buum
avoid the unusual word as if it were a cliff

Advice to orators from Caesar, and good advice it is for those who want to be understood and convince others.

V

vale
WAH-lay
farewell

vectigalia nervi sunt rei publicae
wayk-tee-GAAH-lih-yah NEHR-wee suunt RAY-yee POO-blih-kī
taxes are the sinews of the state

The words of Cicero, who knew how much war and other state activities cost. Today's politicians are not always bold enough to say this. (See also NERVI BELLI, PECUNIA INFINITA.)

vel prece vel pretio
wehl PREH-keh wehl PREH-tih-yoh
for love or money

Literally "either by entreaty or by bribe." (See also NEC PRECE NEC PRETIO.)

veluti in speculum
WEH-luu-tee ihn SPEH-kuu-luum
you're one too

This rejoinder, literally "just as if in a mirror," is appropriate when reference is made to one's own faults. (See also TAMQUAM IN SPECULUM.)

venalis populus, venalis curia patrum
way-NAAH-lihs PAW-puu-luus way-NAAH-lihs KOO-rih-yah PAH-truum
everyone has a price

Literally "the people are venal, and the senate is equally venal." This was said of the Roman Senate, and some believe that nothing much has changed over the centuries.

vendidit hic auro patriam
WEHN-dih-diht hihk OW-roh PAH-trih-yahm
this man sold his country for gold

Virgil excoriating a traitor.

veniam pro laude peto
WEH-nih-yahm proh LOW-deh PEH-toh
just give me a chance to be heard

Ovid addressing his critics, literally "I seek indulgence rather than praise."

venia necessitati datur
WEH-nih-yah neh-kehs-sih-TAAH-tee DAH-tuur
we show kindness to those who are truly in need

Literally "indulgence is granted to necessity." Or so we like to think. (See also NECESSITAS NON HABET LEGEM.)

venienti occurrite morbo
weh-nih-YEHN-tee awk-KUUR-rih-teh MAWR-boh
an ounce of prevention is worth a pound of cure

Persius encouraging preventive medicine with the literal injunction: "forestall oncoming disease." But what Persius told us can apply to other threats to our well-being as well as to life and limb.

venit summa dies et ineluctabile tempus
WAY-niht SUUM-mah DIH-yays eht ihn-ay-look-TAAH-bih-leh TEHM-puus

here comes big trouble for the Dow Jones average

Virgil, seeing that the fall of Troy was imminent, has given prophets of doom the right words to use in sounding the death knell, literally "the final day has come and the inescapable moment."

venter non habet aures
WEHN-tehr nohn HAH-beht OW-rays

don't preach to a starving family

Literally "the belly has no ears." It takes more than words to satisfy hungry people.

ventis secundis
WEHN-tees seh-KUUN-dees

when things are going your way

Literally "with favorable winds."

vera incessu patuit dea
WAY-rah ihn-KEHS-soo PAH-tuu-wiht DEH-yah

She walks in beauty, like the night
Of cloudless climes and starry skies

While not matching Lord Byron in metaphoric grandeur, Virgil tells us "she walked with the dignity of a goddess," literally "by her gait the true goddess was revealed."

verbera, sed audi
WEHR-beh-raah sehd OW-dee

don't shoot the messenger

Literally "beat me, but hear me out."

vere scire est per causas scire
WAY-ray SKEE-reh ehst pehr KOW-saahs SKEE-reh
you have to get to the bottom of things

Literally "to know truly is to know causes"; more freely "real knowledge lies in understanding causes."

veritas nihil veretur nisi abscondi
WAY-rih-taahs NIH-hihl weh-RAY-tuur NIH-sih ahb-SKAWN-dee
truth fears nothing but concealment

See also OBSCURIS VERA INVOLVENS.

veritas praevalebit
WAY-rih-taahs prī-wah-LAY-biht
truth will prevail

Usually.

veritas temporis filia
WAY-rih-taahs TEHM-paw-rihs FEE-lih-yah
the truth will out

It just takes a bit of time, literally "truth is the daughter of time." (See also VERITATEM DIES APERIT.)

veritatem dies aperit
way-rih-TAAH-tehm DIH-yays AH-peh-riht
time reveals the truth

See also VERITAS TEMPORIS FILIA.

ver perpetuum
wayr pehr-PEH-tuu-wuum
perpetual spring

We can always look forward to a fresh start.

vestigia morientis libertatis
wehs-TEE-gih-yah maw-rih-YEHN-tihs lee-behr-TAAH-tihs
the footprints of expiring liberty

We ignore such signs at great peril to society.

vestis virum facit
WEHS-tihs WIH-ruum FAH-kiht
clothes make the man

veteris vestigia flammae
WEH-teh-rees wehs-TEE-gih-yah FLAHM-mī
traces of that old flame

Virgil commenting on Dido's passion for Aeneas. Dido was the queen of Carthage who fell in love with Aeneas when he was shipwrecked and committed herself to the flames after he left Carthage. Talk about old flames! This was the original.

vexata quaestio
wayks-AAH-tah KWĪS-tih-yoh
a vexing or distressing question

Also given as QUAESTIO VEXATA.

victrix fortunae sapientia
WEEK-treeks fawr-TOO-nī sah-pih-YEHN-tih-yah
wisdom is the winner over good luck

Juvenal had this right, at least in the long run.

vide et crede
WIH-day eht KRAY-deh
see and believe

We are being told to believe our eyes.

videtur
wih-DAY-tuur
it appears *or* it seems

vigilantibus, non dormientibus, iura (or jura) subveniunt
wih-gih-LAHN-tih-buus nohn dawr-mih-YEHN-tih-buus YOO-rah suub-WEH-nih-yuunt
laws help the watchful, not the sleeping

So be alert to what laws allow—and do not allow. Otherwise, you will not know what your rights and restrictions are.

vile donum, vilis gratia
WEE-leh DOH-nuum WEE-lihs GRAAH-tih-yah
poor gift, poor thanks

It's not the thought that counts? Better shop at Tiffany's.

vilius argentum est auro, virtutibus aurum
WEE-lih-yuus ahr-GEHN-tuum ehst OW-roh wihr-TOO-tih-buus OW-ruum
money isn't everything

Horace telling us literally "silver is of less value than gold, gold less than virtue."

vincere aut mori
WIHN-keh-reh owt MAW-ree
to conquer or die

vino tortus et ira
WEE-noh TAWR-tuus eht EE-raah
racked by wine and anger

Horace's characterization of a pugnacious drunk.

vino vendibili hedera non opus est
WEE-noh wehn-DIH-bih-lee HEH-deh-rah nohn AW-puus ehst
word of mouth may be all you need

Literally "a popular wine needs no ivy." Ivy was sacred to Bacchus, a Greek god of wine, so the ivy bush was displayed on signs outside Roman taverns. To demonstrate that old ways do not die easily, an English proverb dating back to the sixteenth century has it that "good wine needs no bush."

vires acquirit cundo
WEE-rays ahk-KWEE-riht eh-YUUN-doh
once a story finds its legs, it's hard to stop

Virgil, speaking of rumor or gossip, tells us literally "it gains strength as it goes." (See also FAMA NIHIL EST CELERIUS.)

virescit vulnere virtus
wih-RAYS-kiht WUUL-neh-reh WIHR-toos
courage flourishes from a wound

And that's why even severely wounded soldiers have been known to continue to fight, performing acts of heroism well above and beyond the call of duty.

virtus ariete fortior
WIHR-toos ah-RIH-yeh-teh FAWR-tih-yawr
virtue is stronger than a battering ram

Virtus, "virtue," here may also be interpreted as "valor" or as "heroism."

virtus in actione consistit
WIHR-toos ihn aahk-tih-YOH-neh kohn-SIHS-tiht
valor lies in action

Not in words.

virtus incendit vires
WIHR-toos ihn-KEHN-diht WEE-rays
courage rouses one's strength

virtus vincit invidiam
WIHR-toos WIHN-kiht ihn-WIH-dih-yahm
virtue overcomes envy

virtute et fide
wihr-TOO-teh eht FIH-day
by virtue and faith

virtute non astutia
wihr-TOO-teh nohn ahs-TOO-tih-yah
by excellence, not by cunning

virtute non verbis
wihr-TOO-teh nohn WEHR-bees
by virtue, not by words

virtuti non armis fido
wihr-TOO-tee nohn AHR-mees FEE-doh
I trust to virtue, not to arms

virum volitare per ora
WIH-ruum waw-lih-TAAH-reh pehr OH-rah
to spread like wildfire

Literally "to fly through the mouths of men." The allusion is to gossip, rumor, and news.

vis a fronte
wees aah FRAWN-teh
a propelling force from in front

vis a tergo
wees aah TEHR-goh
a propelling force from behind

vis comica
wees KOH-mih-kah
comic power *or* comic talent

vis conservatrix naturae
wees kohn-sehr-WAAH-treeks
naah-TOO-rī
the preserving power of nature

See also VIS MEDICATRIX NATURAE.

vis inertiae
wees ih-NEHR-tih-yī
passive resistance to force applied

Literally "the power of idleness."

vis maior (or **major**)
wees MAH-yawr
greater force *or* superior force

A legal term denoting circumstances beyond one's control.

vis medicatrix naturae
wees meh-dih-KAAH-treeks naah-TOO-rī
the healing power of nature

See also VIS CONSERVATRIX NATURAE.

vitae praecepta beatae
WEE-tī prī-KEHP-tah beh-YAAH-tī
directions for a happy life

vitiis nemo sine nascitur
WIH-tih-yees NAY-moh SIH-neh NAAHS-kih-tuur
no one is born without faults

A truth from Horace. (See also ABUNDANT DULCIBUS VITIIS.)

vive memor leti
WEE-weh MEH-mawr LAY-tee
live as though today were your last

Persius telling us soberly and literally "live mindful of death."

vivimus in posteris
WEE-wih-muus ihn PAWS-teh-rees
we live in our posterity

And that's why we must do everything we can to nurture our children and grandchildren. (See also CULPAM MAIORUM POSTERI LUUNT.)

vivit post funera virtus
WEE-wiht pawst FOO-neh-rah WIHR-toos
your good deeds won't be forgotten

Literally "excellence survives the grave."

volat hora per orbem
WAW-laht HOH-rah pehr AWR-behm
time flies

Literally "time flies through the world." Also given as **tempus fugit** (TEHM-puus FUU-giht), "time flies."

voluptates corporis
waw-luup-TAAH-tays KAWR-paw-rihs
sensual pleasures

Literally "the pleasures of the body."

volventibus annis
wawl-WEHN-tih-buus AHN-nees
as time goes by

Virgil observing the passage of time, literally "with the years rolling on."

vox faucibus haesit
wohks FOW-kih-buus HĪ-siht
he was struck dumb

Virgil giving us his version of how it feels to find yourself speechless with amazement, literally "the voice stuck in the throat."

vox stellarum
wohks stayl-LAAH-ruum
the music of the spheres

Literally "the voice of the stars."

vulgus ignobile
WUUL-guus ihg-NOH-bih-leh
the low-born rabble

vulnus immedicabile
WUUL-nuus ihm-meh-dih-KAAH-bih-leh
an incurable wound

English Index

every last one of us should speak and write correctly, 52

every lover is out of his (or her) mind, 186

every lover serves as a soldier, 158

everyone has a price, 261

everyone is equal before the law, 144

everyone is the architect of his or her own success, 109

everyone's home is his (or her) safest refuge, 92

everything depends on having a good reputation, 242

everything that is born passes away, 85

everything unknown is thought magnificent, 206

every vice is downhill, 185

evil intent, 153

from evil intent, 85

examples are odious, 104

excellence survives the grave, 269

excepting what is to be excepted, 104

due exceptions being made, 104

excerpts, 104

from excessive caution, 103

excusable neglect, 78

execution by hanging, 247

expectation of gain, 183

experience bought with pain teaches effectively, 96

the experienced person is apprehensive, 107

experience is the best teacher, 258

experience teaches, 107

experience will teach you many things, 258

expertly, 227

the experts should be trusted in their own areas of competence, 197

to explain one obscurity by another, 145

in explicit terms, 107

exploits, 220

extend a hand to the needy, 80

extermination, 14

extracts, 104

the extreme, 12

to the eyes, 17

in the eyes of citizens, 136

F

facts, 220

to fail when on the verge of success, 165

faith creates faith, 115

to the faithful, 12

faithful and bold, 115

faithful to my unhappy country, 193

faithful to the end, 12

faithful to the (funerary) urn, 114

faith is stronger than a lion, 144

false in one thing, false in everything, 112

false modesty, 153

fame isn't everything, 168

far be it (from me)!, 146

farewell, 260

fast enough if safely enough, 226

fast enough if well enough, 226

the fates lead the willing, drag the unwilling, 92

a fault is nourished and lives by being concealed, 24

favorable things, 221

with favorable winds, 262

fear, all-powerful fear, 253

fear betrays base souls, 86

fear created the gods, 253

fear God, honor the king, 252

fear has added wings to one's feet, 195

I

it is a bad plan that cannot be changed, 152

it is as well to try, 45

it is crushed by its own weight, 159

it is fitting that an emperor die standing, 84

it is not proper, 176

it is the heart that makes persons eloquent, 194

it is unnatural, 187

it is worthwhile, 187

it lacks beginning and end, 57

I too have been in Arcadia, 100

I trust and am at peace, 67

I trust to virtue, not to arms, 267

it's all over for us, 10

it's all over with the commonwealth, 10

it's a mistake to flaunt your wealth, 47

it's a new ball game every time, 179

it's a very good thing to enjoy the folly of others, 22

it's best to sleep on the matter, 136

it's better not to suffer personal attacks in silence, 248

it's easy to add to things already invented, 110

it's easy to be generous with another person's property, 110

it's easy to shout "kill him" from ringside, 244

it's easy to talk a good game, 137

it seems, 265

it's hard to deal with closet enemies, 247

it shines with another's light, 147

it's not at all easy to fly without wings, 237

it's OK to shoot someone who's pointing a gun at you, 36

it's one thing to conceal, another to be silent, 25

it's pleasant when safe on land to watch the great struggle of another out on a swelling sea, amid winds churning the deep, 244

it's pointless to run in place, 212

it's the thought behind a gift that counts, 8

I've got a tiger by the tail, 40

I was only following orders, 10

I will cut this man's throat with his own sword, 246

I will keep the faith, 233

I wrap myself up in my virtue, 155

I wrote these insignificant lines of verse, another person took the credit, 128

I yield to a superior, 151

J

jack-of-all-trades, master of none, 24

Jehovah breathed and they were dispersed, 20

Jesus Christ, 148

jokes that hurt aren't funny, 176

the joys of battle, 61

judge a tree by its fruit, not by its leaves, 117

judge by results, not by appearances, 117

the judge is condemned when a criminal is set free, 139

I'm just an average Joe, not an eye surgeon, 82

just as if in a mirror, 260

just before daybreak, 33

just behave yourself, 42

just for appearances, 204

W

the wagon drags the ox, 80

wall, 138

war is neither to be feared nor to be provoked, 44

war is profitable for many, 162

warmed-over cabbage, 74

war memorial, 65

war profiteering is nothing new, 162

the war of all against all, 44

a war of extermination, 44

watch out especially for the people close to you, 216

watch out for economists, racetrack touts, and meteorologists, 46

watch out for snoopers, 196

watch out for the know-it-all, 197

watch what you say, 102

the way must be tried, 251

the way to get ahead, 11

the way to go, 45

we all have our own quirks, 254

we all must die one day, 194

wealth is not an unmixed blessing, 149

we are all impelled by a desire to be praised, and the higher a man's standing, the more he is deceived by glory, 254

we are always striving for what is forbidden, and desiring what is denied us, 173

we are but dust and shadow, 205

we are destined for death, we and our works, 83

to the wearied the ground is a bed, 112

to wear two hats, 92

a weary traveler, 113

we being judges, 174

we can count many friends when we are successful, 250

we catchers have been caught, 56

we conquer by degrees, 119

wedge drives wedge, 79

we grow slowly, die quickly, 73

we learn from experience, 107

we live in our posterity, 269

we live more by example than by reason, 105

well born, well dressed, and so-so in learning, 46

to the well-deserving, 45

well-disposed to virtue alone and to its friends, 256

well has he lived who has lived in obscurity, 47

a well-matched pair, 191

we readily believe what we wish to believe, 215

we shall overcome, 165

we show kindness to those who are truly in need, 261

we want him (or her) on our side, 251

what a woman says to an ardent lover should be written on wind and running water, 161

what does this mean?, 209

what do you fear?, 211

whatever folly their rulers commit, the Greeks suffer the penalty, 210

whatever is done for good men is never lost, 49

whatever you do, don't stonewall, 24

whatever you're trying to teach us, be brief, 209

what good does it do?, 210

what good is health if you can't afford to enjoy it?, 73

and what had been only a footpath became a highway, 102